Missak Khralian

PALAHOVID

AN ANCESTRAL MEMOIR

(An Armenian Orphan's Experiences of Terror
During the Extermination of Armenians)

Translated from Armenian by Simon Beugekian
Edited with an introduction by Ara Sarafian

Gomidas Institute
London

The Gomidas Institute would like to thank Missak and Sara Khralian's children, Yvette, Alain, Aris, Jean (deceased) and Georgette (Choragat or Shoghagat), as well as their grandson Thierry Karibian, for allowing the publication of this English translation of *Palahovid: An Ancestral Memoir*.

This translation was made possible by the Ararat Eskijian Museum and Mr. and Mrs. Greg & Nora Mazmanian.

© 2021 Gomidas Institute. All Rights Reserved.

ISBN 978-1-903656-63-3

For more information please contact
Gomidas Institute
42 Blythe Rd.
London, W14 0HA
ENGLAND

Email: *info@gomidas.org*
Web: *www.gomidas.org*

*To the people of Palahovid and
those who perished in 1915*

From the Publishers

This work is a complete English translation of Missak Khralian's memoir, Բալահովիտ (հայ որբի մը ապրումները հայաջինջ սարսափներէն) հայրենի յիշատակարան [*Palahovid (hay vorpi mu abroumneru hayachinch sarsapneren) hayreni hishadagaran*] which was originally printed in 1938 by Masis Press in Sofia (Bulgaria). The English translation of this work is *Palahovid: An Ancestral Memoir (An Armenian Orphan's Experiences of Terror during the Extermination of Armenians)*.

This translation includes all illustrations and captions of the original Armenian work. However, we have replaced the photograph of Palou Bridge with the same but better quality stock image courtesy Project Save Archives.

This work uses western Armenian for the transliteration of proper nouns.

All footnotes are those of the editor.

Photograph and Illustration Credits

p. vi, Gomidas Institute. Map based on *Armenians in Palou (1915)*, color map, London: Gomidas Institute, 2021.

p. viii, Gomidas Institute, *Armenian Genocide: Deportation and Massacre Routes through Palahovid (Palou) c. 1915*.

p. x, "An aerial view of the town of Palou before WWI" in Victor Pietschmann *Durch kurdische Berge und armenische Städte Tagebuch d. österr. Armenienexpedition 1914*, Vienna: Adolph Luse Verlag, 1940, p. 161 (plate).

p. xiii, "Group of Armenian orphan refugees as they are forced to leave their native lands, Mezire, 22 Oct. 1922," Vahe Hayg (comp. and ed.), *Kharpert yev Anor Vosgeghen Tashdu: Houshamadyan Badmagan, Mshagoutayin yev Azkakragan*, [s.n.]: New York, 1959, p. 1465.

Background cover image: The Aradzani or Eastern Euphrates flowing westwards of Palou town. The village of Til is 10 miles downstream. Photograph taken on the eve of WWI. Source: Victor Pietschmann, Durch kurdische Berge, Vienna: Adolph Luse Verlag, 1940.

TABLE OF CONTENTS

Introduction   vii

Preface   5

PALAHOVID
Part A: A Chronicle of the Homeland

    A General Overview   7
    1760-1915   11
    First Memories   20
    Persecution   25
    Conscription and Exile   32
    A Page from the Bloody Year of 1915   61

Part B: The Horrors Experienced during the Extermination of Armenians

    "Yev Yeghev Souk"   73
    "Mayig… Chem Gna… Shad en…"   77
    "I Weep… But I Succeed…"   81
    My First Heartbeat…   90
    Forced to Record Death Sentences   100
    An Invisible Hand at Work   106
    A Visitor in the Night   108
    The Haven of Mercy   116

[Part C] A Historical Overview

    A Bit of History   139

    Melkon Gurjian   147

History and Traditions

    Short Remarks on Palou   149
    Islamized Begs   150
    Some Examples of Traditions   151
    The Monastery   154

    To the New Generation   159

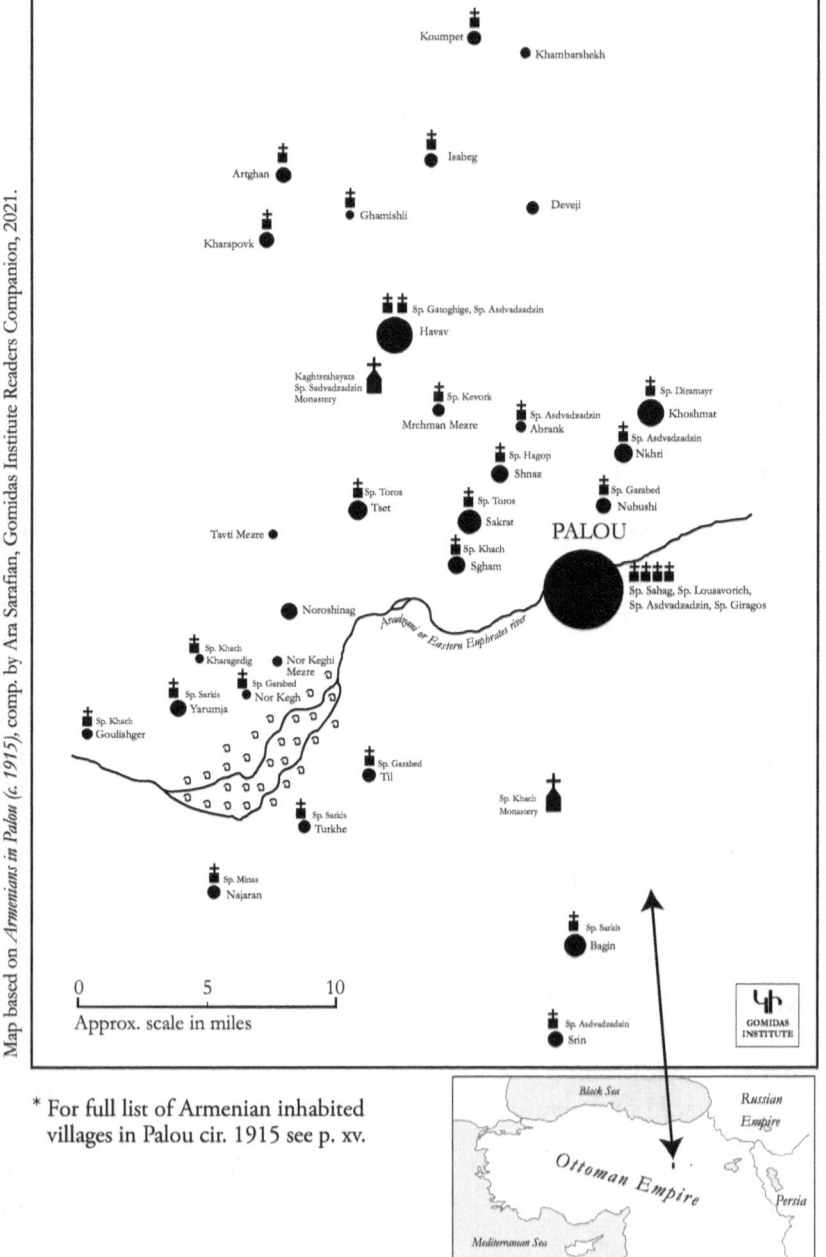

Introduction

Historical Location

Palahovid[1] is the memoir of Missak Khralian, a child survivor of the Armenian Genocide.[2] He was a 14-year-old boy in 1915 when Ottoman authorities embarked on a genocidal campaign to erase the Armenian presence in the Ottoman Empire. Khralian's own ancestral village of Til (in Palahovid or Palou) was one of 40 Armenian settlements targeted for destruction in this district (see table on page xv).[3] It was a small settlement of 25 Armenian households and 10 Kurdish and Turkish ones. The core of his memoir covers the years between 1914 and 1922.[4] It is a powerful work of seminal importance.[5]

Khralian's account of the destruction of Armenians falls into a classic sequence of events that came to define the Armenian Genocide in the eastern provinces of the Ottoman Empire.[6] It includes the vilification of Armenians through state propaganda and malicious rumors;[7] the occupation of Til by paramilitary and government forces;[8] the arrest and execution of Armenian men, including the author's father and uncles;[9] the mass deportation of women and children following the murder of the men;[10] and the abduction of around 20 women and children for absorption into Muslim households. All of these developments took place in rapid succession in June-July 1915.

Khralian was one of the children who were held back for assimilation into the Muslim community. He had to convert to Islam, change his name, and deny his Armenian identity.[11] He soon became a servant and cowherd to Hashim Beg, the local Kurdish overlord. His duties as a cowherd required him to move about Til and surrounding areas with his animals, thus allowing him the ability to make observations and gather information on Armenians. Perhaps most remarkably, he also worked as a messenger for Hashim Beg and was permitted to enter his master's women's quarter (harem), where he communicated with captive Armenian women. He thus gives us invaluable insights into the lives of several of these women and their ultimate fates.

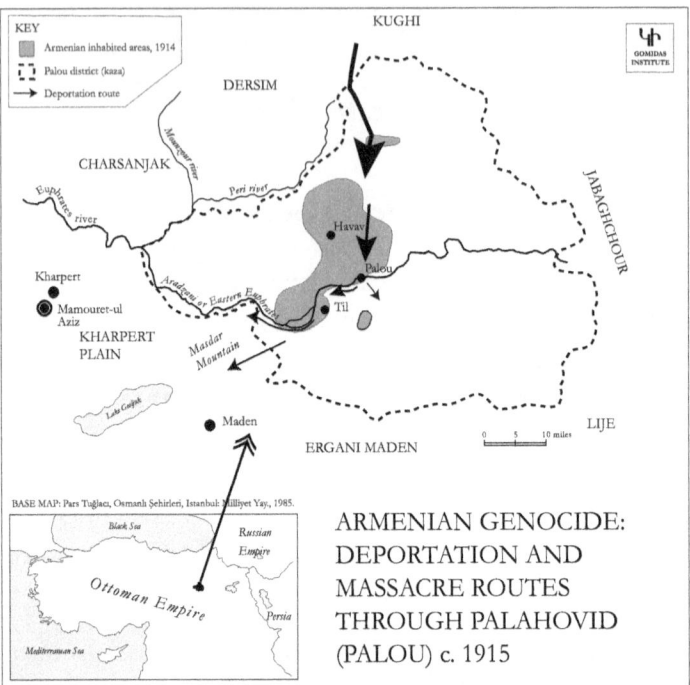

Broad Observations and Concrete Cases

Khralian relates his testimony regarding the Armenian Genocide in terms of broad observations and concrete examples. While he reports the mass arrest and execution of Armenian men, he describes his last, heartrending meeting with his father, as well as his examination of his father's corpse outside the village after the men had been killed.[12] He describes the horrors of deportations and the terrorized state of Armenians, including the case of a desperate woman drowning her youngest child so that the rest of the family would have a better chance of surviving so-called deportations (i.e. death marches) to the deserts of Syria.[13] His description includes his own role in drowning that two year-old child.[14] Similarly, he makes references to widespread violence in the village and gives detailed accounts of the merciless beatings he received.[15] On one occasion, he was beaten and kicked in the head as he lay motionless on the ground.[16] He had been suffering from typhoid fever at the time.[17]

Khralian's account touches on the particular victimization of Armenian women after July 1915. One victim, Satenig, was originally from Til and placed in Hashim Beg's harem when the killings and abuses started.

Introduction

Khralian describes how she was groomed for assimilation while the older Armenian women around her, also in the harem, urged the author to claim her hand in marriage. After all, he and Satenig knew each other, and, as he had already converted to Islam, their marriage would have saved her from the looming terrible prospects. However, the idea that he could marry Satenig seemed absurd to Khralian, given his terrible physical state (he was clad in rags, malnourished, and terrorized by others), the ongoing murder of Armenians around him, and the number of Kurds interested in her. When Satenig was eventually taken by a Kurdish man in Til, Khralian kept an eye on her from a distance, until she disappeared one day, undoubtedly murdered by her captor.[18]

Another young woman who perished in Til was Shoghagat, originally from Trabizon.[19] The men in her family had been taken away and presumably killed in the initial stages of deportations, while she was sent off with her mother and sister Sirarpi to the deserts of Syria. Her sister was abducted during an attack on their deportation convoy at Palou bridge, a few hours from Til.[20] As the convoy continued after the attack, Shoghagat and her mother were picked out of their convoy near Til. The two women were placed in Hashim Beg's harem, where Shoghagat also entered the grooming process and was expected to convert to Islam, renounce her identity, and become a Turk. However, since she did not submit to expectations, she simply disappeared one day. She was apparently taken by Nejib Beg who abused her with his friends at his "ghonakh" (so-called mansion) between the villages of Turkhe and Alkhatian. Khralian eventually buried her unborn child, and later, Shoghagat as well.[21] Khralian later named one of his own daughters, born in France, after her.[22]

In another case, Khralian describes the murder of Oghida, his cousin's wife, who had been forced into marriage with a Kurd from Meyman. One day, while grazing his animals, Khralian discovers Oghida's corpse outside Til. She had been gagged and tortured before being killed. According to Khralian, she had probably escaped from Meyman and wanted to return to her home, before being apprehended and killed by her captor.[23]

Not all Armenian women abducted during this period were killed. The author's paternal-uncle Vartan's wife, Sara, was married to a Kurdish man after her Armenian husband was murdered alongside the other men of Til in June 1915.[24] Another female relative, Oskeg, was married to a Kurdish

An aerial view of the town of Palou before WWI. Palou bridge is in the distance to the left.

man in Turkhe and bore him two sons by 1921.²⁵ Khralian's description of his final parting from Oskeg is heartbreaking.²⁶

Most victims and victimizers in Til knew each other, and Khralian's descriptions of his victimizers are particularly telling. He provides vivid pictures of Hashim Beg, his character, facial features and personal conduct.²⁷ At one point, he states how some of the local murderers bragged about the number of Armenians they had raped and killed. One mass murderer and rapist, Arif Agha of Anatots village, claimed 95 victims, while another, Siusli Hasan of Til, bragged of 122 victims.²⁸ According to Khralian, there was only one Kurdish family in Til, Bukoyents Msto, that refused to have any part in the abuses that were taking place. Khralian was consoled by the fact that Msto's family looked after his younger brother, Setrag.²⁹

Khralian survived the Armenian Genocide because of a number of factors, such as his age, gender, presence of mind and luck. He was old enough to understand what was going on around him, yet young enough not to be killed outright like the other men and older boys in the village. He was also lucky to be taken into captivity instead of being deported and probably killed, even if he had to endure severe beatings, ruthless exploitation, mental torture and starvation in the village. The fact that his tasks included looking after cattle (stolen from Armenians) allowed him to meet up with other Armenian cowherds, forage for food, and even contemplate escape.[30] Other victims, such as Sara, Oghida, Shoghagat, Satenig or Oskeg, were trapped in Muslim households, with little room to maneuver. Some of them were killed; others were absorbed into Muslim households; and a few managed to escape at the end of World War I. Khralian does not reflect on the fate of younger children other than his own brother and niece, Setrag and Jouhar.[32]

All of the killings and abuses Khraian witnessed were organized or sanctioned by Ottoman officials and carried out with the support of local Muslim Turks and Kurds. He saw gendarmes who led deportation convoys visit Hashim Beg in Til and discuss their activities at his "ghonakh."[31] Khralian even describes what he saw of torture, rape and murder committed by such officials.[33] At one point, in fall 1915, Hashim Beg and some officials even wanted Khralian to undertake a headcount of surviving Armenian women in Til so that those who had not been taken by Muslim men could be deported.[34] Khralian managed to avoid drawing up such a "death sentence,"[35] though the deportation of such women went forth, anyway.[36]

Authentic Account, Warts and All

Much of Khralian's account is choppy and was probably written at different times. We can presume he wrote his recollections entirely from memory in the 1930s.[37] His work was clearly not edited for style or content and therefore has a certain authentic, raw quality as a primary source. Even the order of sections in the book is problematic, with the historical background appearing after the core of the memoir on the Armenian Genocide. His account could be considered a first or second draft of his work, still in the voice of the author, and in many ways more amenable to our critical appraisal.

The time markers in his account are not always clear. Events are most often presented with reference to each other, with occasional clues in terms of seasons, weather or harvests. Some dates are seemingly wrong. For example, the author states that his great-grandfather came to Til as a young man in his 20s before 1760. That date seems unlikely given the ages of his great-grandfather, grandfather and father's generation. He also mentions that his great-grandfather and his sons had dealings with Sultan Abdul-Aziz who reigned between 1861-86. His great-grandfather probably came to Til prior to the 1860s and not the 1760s.[38]

While Khralian states that he was 14 years old in 1915 – and he very well may have been – he also refers to his age elsewhere as barely 10 years old at that time.[39]

The core of the memoir, about the Armenian Genocide, seems to have been written twice without being integrated into a single narrative. The first section starts before 1915 and ends in 1918, while the second section starts in 1915 and ends in 1922.[40] Although the second section was written to supplement the first one, a number of significant themes remain divided into the two parts. Perhaps the most important such theme concerns the fate of the author's father in 1915. While the first section describes his arrest and imprisonment, the second section describes his murder – 35 pages later.[41]

Two prominent victims, Shoghagat and Satenig, appear separately, one in the first section, the other in the second. Yet it is not clear which one figures in Khralian's chronology first. It was probably Satenig, who appears in the second section.

Khralian also repeats some unlikely scenarios he had heard, or so he thought, as facts. He states that Shoghagat's fiancé had fled to the Caucasus when Armenian soldiers were disarmed in the Ottoman army [February 1915] and then returned to Trabizon to organise his wedding with Shoghagat, only to be deported less than two months later.[42] If Shoghagat's fiancé had served in the Ottoman army and fled to the Caucasus, it is unlikely that he would have returned as a deserter to organise a wedding during wartime. Khralian also states that Ottoman soldiers who deserted the army three times were shot.[43] Again, it is unlikely that such soldiers were not shot the first time they deserted and were apprehended. Such elements of the memoir reflect the author's innocence when writing his memoir. One of the more bizarre episodes he describes, at some length, concerns the appearance of an armed Armenian, or a group of Armenians, who came to Til in order to rescue an Armenian woman, originally from Baghin, with the help of sympathetic Ottoman officials in Diyarbakir – possibly in Mifarghin or Farghin, modern day Silvan.[44] The story sounds delusional, especially in the wake of the author's ailment from typhoid fever and a severe beating at the time, were it not for the detailed description he provides.

The only jarring element in the memoir is an odd contradiction. In the first section of the core narrative, the author states that he was in Til until 1918, when he left the village and sought his freedom.[45] This section was obviously written first, possibly as a standalone abridged account, and then included in the full memoir without correction. However, in the second section of the core narrative, Khralian details how he actually fled to Kharpert in the winter of 1916-17, where he was adopted by a Turkish family and remained with them for three years.[46] He then returned to Til in October 1920 to look for surviving members of his family. This return was after the Ottoman defeat in WWI and prior to the rise of the Kemalist Turks and the establishment of the Turkish Republic. Finding his brother, stepmother, a cousin and a niece, as well as more distant relations, he made amends with Hashim Beg and settled down in the village.[47] However, his return was short lived as he was forced out by Hashim Beg, along with several of his surviving relatives, under very distressing circumstances in late 1921 or early 1922.[48] Khralian went to Kharpert again and sheltered at the Armenian prelacy and orphanage. He was there for 10 months and left during the general evacuation of Armenian orphans from the region at the end of 1922.[49] His journey took him to Aleppo, Beirut and eventually, Marseille, in 1925.

A Legacy of Pain and Injustice

This memoir is an intimate eye-witness account of the Armenian Genocide. It was written 20 years after the events in question and reflected on the author's experiences, as well as those of others. Khralian's suffering was comparable to those of tens of thousands of other Armenian children who were abducted during the Armenian Genocide of 1915. Some of them managed to survive and escape, others were assimilated into Muslim families, and many were simply killed.

Khralian wrote his memoir as a testimony to his lost world, an ancestral memoir, and called on future generations of Armenians to remember, survive as Armenians, and extract vengeance for the losses of 1915. He dedicated his work to his wife and "the Satenigs and Sophias, who fell to the blows of the Turk without greeting the dawn of freedom."

Group of Armenian orphan refugees as they are forced to leave their native lands, Mezire, 22 Oct. 1922.

His memoir reflected his enduring pain, loss and despair because the world had forgotten, or chose not to remember, the extermination of Armenians. His memoir was published in 1938, a year before Adolph Hitler, pointing to the extermination of Armenians, embarked on another path to war and genocide in the heart of Europe.

Ara Sarafian
Gomidas Institute, London
April 2021

ARMENIAN INHABITED SETTLEMENTS IN PALAHOVID (PALOU)[50]

SETTLEMENT	Armenian households	Armenian individuals	Kurdish individuals	Turkish individuals
Palou	250	1600	500	6000
Havav	207	1618		
Artukhan	33	274	7	
Khamushli [Ghamishli]	9	82		
Isabeg	25	209		
Kiumbet [Koumbat, Kmpet]	32	196	25	
Khambarshekh	4	34	94	
Devedji [Devaji]	4	49	139	
Tepe [Tapa]	61	337	56	
Dilimli	4	51	36	
Grbsi Mezre	6	59	21	
Okhou [Oghou]	25	250	150	
Kharabork [Kharapovk]	21	195	78	
Nubushi	36	279		
Sugham	51	372		
Sakrat	75	650	25	13
Najaran	25	187	32	
Turkhe	32	167	23	
Til	24	155	60	10
Kengerli	28	169		
Khajar	7	56	20	
Giulishger [and its mezre]	27	143	2	
Nor Kiugh	21	98		6
Tset	87	454		
Abrank	23	133		6
Ouzoun Ova	3	178		13
Ouzoun Ova Mezre	9	95		
Khoshmat	114	853	30	10
Halalkom	8	48		
Chayri Mezre	12	126		
Nkhri	62	440		1
Baghin	102	617		
Surin	32	296		
Shnaz	54	374		
Yarumja	30	296		35
Kharagedig	12	94		
Tavti Mezre	10	98		
Mrchman Mezre	20	180		
Ashnkegh	6	116		
Akpounar	3	31	15	
	1,594	11,659	1,313	6,094

Number of Armenian inhabited settlements in district: Town of Palou and 39 villages.

ENDNOTES

1. Palahovid or the valley of Palou in Armenian.
2. This book was originally published by Masis Press (Sofia, Bulgaria) in 1938. A French translation appeared in 2007 under the title, *Les faucilles sanglantes: paroles d'un rescapé du génocide arménien* (Cheminemenys) by Missak Khralian and Thierry Karibian with a preface by Raymond Kevorkian. The present volume is the first English translation of this work.
3. The Palou district (kaza) was part of the province of Diyarbakir in 1915. The Armenian population of this district on the eve of WWI has been estimated between 8,390 and 18,740 people. See Sarkis Y. Karayan, *Armenians in the Ottoman Turkey, 1914: A Geographic and Demographic Gazetteer* (London: Gomidas Institute, 2018), pp. 292-96.
4. This memoir also includes additional supplemental sections concerning the village of Til and the Khralian family.
5. There are a number of memoirs, compatriotic studies and documentary works that relate to the Armenian Genocide in Palou district. For the massacres in the Okhou region in the northern tiers of Armenian villages, see Parounag Topalian, *Hayreni Kiugh Okhou*, Boston: Hayrenik, 1943 pp. 156-73. For the massacre of Armenians in the nearby Peri region (Charsanjak), see Hampartsoum Chitjian, *A Hair's Breadth Away from Death*, London: Gomidas Institute, 2021 (2nd ed). For the massacres in Baghin (near Til), see Baghin Kiughi Verashinadz yev Ousoumnasiradz Mioutiun, *Badmoutiun Baghnadan*, Boston: Hairenik, 1966, pp. 139-159; For Havav village, see Dikran Papazian, *Badmoutiun Palou Havav Kiughi*, Beirut: Mshag, 1960, p. 79. For the massacres in the Nekhri region north of the town of Palou, as well as the killing of deportees along deportation routes, including the large scale killings on Palou bridge, see Amatouni Virabyan (ed.), *Hayots Tseghasbamoutiunu Osmanyan Tourkiayoum: Verabroghneri Vgayoutiunner, Pasdatoughterou Zhoghovadzou, Erzroumi, Kharperti, Diarbekiri, Sepasdiayi, Trabizoni nahankner [yev] Barsgahayk*, Yerevan: Armenian National Archives, 1912, documents 90, 30, 33, 35, 36, 37. For a description of the fate of a deportation caravan from Erzeroum passing through the Palou region, see Souren H. Hanessian, *Through The Depths: A True Life Story*, London: Gomidas Institute, 2017. For a devastating account of the genocide by another child-survivor, whose odyssey started in his native town of Hoshe and ended up in a village a stone's throw from Til, see Melkon Derderian in Agheden Verabroghner, *Der Zor*, comp. and ed. Levon Mesrob, Paris: Elegian Press, 1955, pp. 289-290; For an incredible account of an Armenian officer in the Ottoman army, who passed through this region in 1916 and describes the devastation of Armenian villages and remaining women and children, see Sarkis Boghosian, *Trkahay Sbayi Mu Orakiru*, Paris: Imp. Araxes, 1941, vol. 2, pp. 73-80, 91-95.
6. For a regional analysis of the Armenian Genocide, including differences and

commonalities across regions, see the 1916 British Parliamentary Blue Book on the Armenian Genocide. James Bryce and Arnold Toynbee, *The Treatment of Armenians in the Ottoman Empire, 1915-16: Documents Presented to Viscount Grey of Fallodon by Viscount Bryce* [Uncensored Edition], edited and with an introduction by Ara Sarafian, London: Gomidas Institute, 2005.

7. While Armenians were vilified in general, there were specific rumours about his family owning a secret weapon that fired bullets the size of crows' eggs and exploded silently, releasing poison into the air. *Palahovid*, p. 65.

8. *Palahovid*, p. 65. Such concerted attacks also took place in other Armenian inhabited villages in Palou and surrounding districts. See *Badmoutiun Baghnadan*, pp. 139-159; *Badmoutiun Palou Havav Kiughi*, p. 79; Hampartzoum Kasbarian, *Chmshgadzak yev ir Kiugher*, Boston, Baikar, 1969, pp. 397-410; *A Hair's Breadth Away from Death*, pp. 88-96; *Der Zor*, pp. 289-90.

9. *Palahovid*, pp. 34-36 and pp. 67, 69-70.

10. *Palahovid*, pp. 38-40 and pp. 108-09. In a special survey carried out for Talaat Pasha in 1917, most Armenians from Diyarbakir province (which included Palou) had disappeared. Of the 56,166 Armenians from Diyarbakir province (official figures), 1,849 survived in February 1917 in the so-called resettlement zones of the Empire. See Talaat Pasha's Report on the Armenian Genocide, comp. ed. and intro. by Ara Sarafian, London: Gomidas Institute, 2011.

11. *Palahovid*, p. 75, 78.

12. *Palahovid*, p. discovery of father's corpse.

13. Her husband was presumably killed in the earlier massacre of Armenian men in the village and she had to leave the village with her children on her own. Practically all deportees in Diyarbakir province were killed in 1915. According to a summary report for Talaat Pasha, 97% of Armenians in this province could not be accounted for at the beginning of 1917. See *Talaat Pasha's Report on the Armenian Genocide*, ed. and intro. by Ara Sarafian, (Gomidas Institute), 2011, p. 57.

14. *Palahovid*, pp. 39-40.

15. *Palahovid*, pp. 41-42, 76, 112, 136-37.

16. *Palahovid*, p. 112.

17. *Palahovid*, p. 110.

18. *Palahovid*, pp. 92-102.

19. *Palahovid*, p. 46-47. Most deportees passing through the district of Palou were either from the Palou region or the neighboring district of Kughi. However, there were some caravans from further north, such as Souren Hanessian's convoy, which was from Erzeroum. See Souren H. Hanessian, *Through The Depths: A True Life Story*, London: Gomidas Institute, 2017.

20. *Palahovid*, pp. 46-47. Palou bridge was a major massacre site, where thousands of Armenians perished in systematic abuses and outright massacres. For detailed eyewitness accounts of such massacres at Palou bridge see See Virabyan, *Hayots Tseghasbanoutiunu...* documents 90, 30, 33, 35, 36, 37.

21. *Palahovid*, pp. 45-61.

22. *Palahovid*, p. 3.

23. *Palahovid*, pp. 95-97.
24. *Palahovid*, pp. 68, 128
25. *Palahovid*, pp. 138-39.
26. *Palahovid*, p. 139.
27. *Palahovid*, p. 103, 136.
28. *Palahovid*, p. 56.
29. *Palahovid*, p. 76-77.
30. *Palahovid*, p. 94.
31. A large number of Armenian women and children were "collected" in Kharpert (Harpoot) by Armenian and American philanthropic organizations between the end of WWI and 1922, when the Kemalist Turks took control over this region. A list of 955 such children in the care of Near East Relief identified 144 children, an equal number of boys and girls, from the Palou region. *Gotchnag* (New York), 7 June 1919. For more information see footnote 49.
32. *Palahovid*, pp. 39, 47, 70, 103, 109, 110.
33. *Palahovid*, p. 78.
34. *Palahovid*, pp. 100-04.
35. *Palahovid*, pp. 105.
36. *Palahovid*, pp. 106-07.
37. There is one reference in his work that states that he was writing his memoir in 1933. *Palahovid*, p. 59.
38. In his preface, Khralian states that he was 14 years old when he escaped the "Medz Yeghern of 1915" (p. 5) and says so again at the end of his book (p. 160). However, he also comments that he was barely 10 years old when he saw his father's corpse in 1915 (p. 68). Later on, he describes how he was allowed access to the women's quarter (harem) in Hashim Beg's household as a messenger. He states that he could enter the harem because he was under 15 years old. However, it is more likely that the upper age allowing him entry would have been and he was granted access because he was – or appeared – younger than that age. (p. 43.)
39. *Palahovid*, p. 68.
40. *Palahovid*, Section 1 is from pp. 20-61, section 2 is from pp. 62-138.
41. *Palahovid*, pp. 34-37 and pp. 66, 68-69.
42. *Palahovid*, p. 45.
43. *Palahovid*, p. 62.
44. *Palahovid*, pp. 111-16.
45. *Palahovid*, pp. 59.
46. We can verify that he fled to Kharpert around early 1917 because he mentions seeing two American missionaries, Mr. and Mrs Riggs. *Palahovid*, p. 118. These two missionaries were in Kharpert until early 1917. Mrs. Riggs died at the end of April 1917 and Mr. Riggs had to leave the Ottoman Empire soon afterwards, when the United States entered WWI. He only returned in late March 1919. Khralian also describes thousands of destitute Armenians begging at the doors of foreign missionaries in Kharpert and Mezreh. This also tallies with other primary sources. See Maria Jacobsen, *Diaries of a Danish Missionary: Harpoot, 1907-1919*,

Kristen Vind (transl) and Ara Sarafian (ed and intro) London and Princeton: Gomidas Institute, 2001. He also states that he was in Kharpert for three years between 1917 and 1920. *Palahovid,* p. 123.

47. He came to an accommodation with Hashim Beg by renouncing any claims to his family's stolen properties in Til, except for the broken flour mill, which he repaired and started to operate with his cousin, Markar. *Palahovid,* p. 127.

48. *Palahovid,* pp. 130-35.

49. *Palahovid,* pp. 138-39. For more information about the Armenian Prelacy of Kharpert between 1918 and 1922 see Kiuid Mkhitarian, *Housher yev Verhishoumner (1918-1935),* Antilias, Lebanon: Cilician Catholicosate, 1937. Also see Varteres Mikayel Garougian, *Destiny of the Dzidzernag,* transl. from Armenian and edited by Mariam V. (Garougian) Sahakian, Princeton and London: Gomidas Institute, 2005, pp. 94-144; Maria Jacobsen, *Diaries of a Danish Missionary: Harpoot, 1907-1919,* Kristen Vind (transl) and Ara Sarafian (ed and intro) London and Princeton: Gomidas Institute, 2001; Ruth A. Parmelee, *A Pioneer in the Euphrates Valley,* London: Gomidas Institute, 2002, pp. 40-68.

50. These are the figures for Palou district from the 1913 population survey undertaken by the Armenian Patriarchate of Constantinople. These figures only cover Armenian inhabited settlements in the district. An additional 10% of Armenians from Palou were absent from the region as migrant workers and their families. See Bibliothèque Nubar (AGBU, Paris), Archival records from the Armenian Patriarchate of Constantinople, DOR 3/2, ff. 59-60. According to Sarkis Y. Karayan, the total number of Armenians in this region could have been as high as 18,740 Armenians. See Sarkis Y. Karayan, *Armenians in Ottoman Turkey, 1914: A Geographic and Demographic Gazeteer,* (London: Gomidas Institute, 2018), pp. 292-96.

Missak Khralian

PALAHOVID

AN ANCESTRAL MEMOIR

(An Armenian Orphan's Experiences of Terror
During the Extermination of Armenians)

Missak Khralian, author.

Dedication

To you.

Sara, I dedicate this Odyssey of my life, this bloody chronicle to you. As a wife, you were as faithful and true to me as a Penelope, and a perfect mother to my Adroushan, Arisdages, and Shoghagat.

In the tremors of your voice, I have always heard the terror-stricken shrieks and final gasps of your martyred sisters, the Satenigs and Sophias, who fell to the blows of the Turk without greeting the dawn of freedom.

You inspired me to memorialize your martyred sisters, whose ashes will give birth to many Nemeses to smite the enemies of my people.

To you I dedicate this lamentation.

–Missak Khralian.

Preface

These are the memoirs of an orphan who, at the age of 14, miraculously escaped the Medz Yeghern of 1915 and the blood-soaked blade of the Turks. An orphan who escaped death under the searing sun of the deserts by a hair's breadth, his spirit forever shattered by the memories of his ordeal. This is the authentic account of the life of an Armenian waif who came to age on the bloody road to exile.

Dear reader, would you travel with me to our native world, to the land of our ancestors? Let us visit those monasteries and churches, let us step over the threshold and enter that sweet, familial world. Let us observe the customs and mores of our predecessors; let us hear their groans, their songs, their laughter, their cries, and their weeping.

Careful, because we will also be plunged into a world of savagery. We will be the spectators of unfathomable outrages committed under the cover of darkness. But be brave, and do not turn away from the horror. We will wade through a sea of blood, stepping over the corpses of our fathers and brothers. We will secretly peek into the palaces of the begs, and we will witness the unspeakable barbarity of the beast called man.

We need to bring nothing with us on this journey. Just a handful of tears, if we are still capable of weeping; and just a lament, if our hearts can still wring one out of their depths. We may even encounter some joy and a few smiles along the way.

When the fire began burning, and the entire city was engulfed in flames, I did not escape like Lot. I remained in the conflagration, and with my own eyes witnessed the slaughter and destruction. Like the dervishes of the desert, I measured "the length and breadth of the bloodied road." I witnessed the downfall of glorious temples; I heard the cries of children and the shrieks of their mothers. I walked under the ruthless sun of the desert. The desert sucked away everything I was, sucked it all away like a snake. Now, I stand before the world and tell the tale of my pain.

Marseille, 1938

M. Kh.

PALAHOVID

Part A

A Chronicle of the Homeland

A General Overview

In 1722, Raffi's *Tavit Beg* heralded a new era. With four hundred Armenian warriors, he fought the 16,000-strong army of the Jivanshirs for two days, eventually routing their forces and capturing their weapons and horses.

We are already acquainted with the history of the Armenian nation since Tavit Beg's exploits, with all its ups and downs, with all its glories and tragedies.

As the rule of the Sultans became more brutal, and as they intensified their efforts to drown the nascent free Armenia in its own womb, Armenians reacted by writhing, raging and seething. The "Armenian Question" dominated the political agenda from the Caucasus to Constantinople, the capital of the sultans.

The cup of pain had overflown. It was impossible to continue bearing the cross. The Armenian villager was stripped of his property and dignity. His life was not protected. His wealth had been siphoned into the pockets of the sardars, aghas, begs, officials and all the way down to the lowliest gendarme officer. Meanwhile, he lived in penury. The most unfortunate were those who had beautiful daughters. One day, their daughters would be gone – taken into the harems of begs, aghas, or sheikhs. Courage was needed to rescue the honor of the Armenian nation. There was great demand for a hand that would act under the cover of darkness and terrorize the Turkish beast. Men like Surke and Garo could no longer tolerate Riushdi and Hussein beys enjoying their brides on the night of their honeymoons.

The account that you are about to read is new to the annals of history. It is all true, it is not a fabrication. The land of Armenia has survived harrowing experiences. It is the duty of history to record these events. This account does not describe the events of a particular era. Rather, it is the latest chapter of centuries of bloodshed. Our fathers told us of their lives, too.

Bloodthirsty and cruel begs ruled us since time immemorial. All those who married would have to hand their bride to the beg, on the night of their wedding, so that the latter could enjoy them first.

Roupen had been engaged for seven years. The years flew by and he could not marry his betrothed...

But the beg was an exacting despot. He forced Roupen to get married that summer, without delay. Roupen stalled, pleaded that he could not do it, that he could not afford it, etc....

Roupen faced a terrible quandary. He could not face the storm raging in his heart. The inevitable was looming before him. Finally, he was forced to comply and had his wedding. A black wedding, of course.

The beg owned the reception hall where the wedding celebration took place. He was seated at the head of the table of honor.

As the evening shadows descended, a beggar, in rags and tatters, came down from the mountains and knocked on Roupen's door. He asked, for the love of Christianity and nation, to be given a corner where he could sleep with a roof over his head. He was given a corner in an empty room.

Who was that beggar? His face was scorched by the hot sun and his spirit was tormented by sorrow and grief. He could not sleep. His heart kept racing and he couldn't calm his mind. As the hours passed, he became paler and paler...

At midnight, he rose and paced around the room, his hands on his heart, as if trying to keep a bird from escaping from his chest.

Suddenly, he heard a terrible scream from the adjacent room. It was the scream of a woman in terrible distress. A tragedy was unfolding within those walls. The newly wedded maiden simply wouldn't succumb to the monstrosities of the beg. She was putting up resistance. It was her honor as an Armenian that wouldn't allow her to relent, and she had kept him at bay late into the night. But at the last minute, unable to go on, she fainted and crumpled to the floor.

At that very moment, someone broke down the door of the room and ran in. It was a spirit of the night and he placed himself between the predator and his prey.

"What is this? What's happening?" raged the beg. "Who are you? Why are you disturbing us?"

"Who am I? I? I am justice and vengeance. I'm just a beggar. A spirit of the mountains. Have you not done enough evil? Are you not satisfied with the pain you've inflicted? Are you not satisfied with the souls you've destroyed?"

And unsheathing a dagger from under his rags, he plunged it into the monster's heart, then went on stabbing him all over the body.

"Die, you dog!" he finally spat out and walked out of the room. He roused the whole house and told Roupen to immediately go to the authorities and tell them that someone had broken into the house and killed the beg. He did this to protect the family. But he did not leave the premises until the arrival of the authorities. Then he made his escape into the mountains, fighting his pursuers along the way.

Or so they said…

People called such actions a "revolution," and the brave men who rebelled against the Turks were called *fedayees*. Over time, their numbers grew. They were everywhere, and wherever an injustice was committed, they raised their fists against it. Amidst the prevailing pain or suffering, these *fedayees* were born from the bosom of the people and walked amongst them.

Sasoun, Van, Moush, and Zeitoun became the epicenters of the Armenian revolution. Musa Beg and his ilk, the abductors and defilers of Armenian Giulizars, had to flee all the way back to Constantinople.

But most of the Armenians in the Ottoman Empire were forlorn and helpless. They were incapable of rescuing themselves from their subjugation and slavery.

Meanwhile, Armenian youth were studying in the Caucasus and Russia, detached from the realities of their compatriots. The Loris-Melikovs, the

Lazarovs, and the Shelkovnikovs made several attempts to liberate the Armenians living under the Ottoman yoke, but they failed repeatedly, "disillusioned with that scoundrel of a Tsar."

This was followed by a period of enthusiasm, when the Armenians of the Caucasus took to the arena with devoted and well-prepared cadres. Meetings were held to discuss how to liberate Ottoman Armenia, protests were organized, newspapers established. Revolutionary apostles were sent across the Turkish border and a powerful movement was built. Teams were dispatched to Geneva, London, and Paris to lobby on behalf of Armenians.

The nascent revolution erupted. 1870, 1880, 1890…

Little by little, the ranks of the revolutionaries swelled. The east was in turmoil. Serops, Kevork Chavoushes, Hrayrs, Zhirayrs, Mourads, and Antranigs sacked the villages and cities of erstwhile despots and plunderers. The Khalils were falling to vengeful bullets. The sword of the Armenian revolutionaries was sharp, and woe to anyone who dared take up Khalil's mantle. Woe to them for whom a Mosin bullet was reserved. Woe to the traitors and the informers, the Tavos, the policemen Haji Dikrans. The hand of the revolutionaries meted out their just punishment with great haste.

The Armenagan Party, Hunchagian Party, and Armenian Revolutionary Federation (Dashnak Party) were founded. The gendarmes and tax collectors, terrified of the vengeance of the *fedayees*, would not dare touch a hair on the head of the poor Armenian villagers. The aghas and begs no longer disrupted the work in the fields. The lazy and thieving Hamdos could no longer kill Armenian shepherds in broad daylight and drive their flock away with impunity. They knew that the *fedayees* would hunt them down, just like they had hunted down Abdo.

The capital of the sultans was worried. Sultan Abdul Hamid donned his red mantle and rode into the arena with the "Kahru Tedmir" to snuff out the infant, the revolution, with the support of infamous Armenians, a coterie of effendis at Yildiz and unworthy clergymen.

A general massacre was orchestrated in 1895. They killed everyone – the elderly, women and children indiscriminately. The schools were shut down, the churches pillaged and destroyed, the ancient books and manuscripts burned. All of the eastern provinces were covered in blood. Those who survived were condemned to famine and starvation.

When representatives of foreign governments raised objections to the massacres with the Sultan, he simply replied, *"Asayish berkemal der!"* ("Total calm prevails!") Then, by gathering cringing, Turcophile Armenian pashas and dishonest higher clergymen around him, he had them sign a statement that "Thanks to His Majesty the Sultan, Armenians are now living happily and in comfort." They then went on to shower Sultan Abdul Hamid with praise and blessings. The Sultan, sending this note to foreign governments, assured them that the alarms raised by Armenian peasants were exaggerated, and that his forces were simply getting rid of some trouble makers to ensure the comfort of the people.

This was the situation in all Turkish Armenia or "the provinces," as the residents of urban Constantinople called it.

After this quick historical summary, we now proceed to focus specifically on my region, Palahovid (Palou), and tell the story of not only the horror that befell it, but also singular episodes of valor and resistance.

1760-1915

Sometime before the 1760s, my *hav* (great-grandfather) Hagop left the mountain village of Srin, located three hours south-east of Palou, and settled down in the village of Til. We do not know why he left his native village, but we know one thing – the entirely Armenian-populated villages of Srin and Baghin were surrounded by bandits in the mountains. These surrounding villagers on rocky mountains, not having arable land, were occupied in either animal husbandry or theft, banditry and pillage. The two Armenian villages were constantly harassed and pillaged by surrounding Kurds. Also, because the region was mountainous and did not have enough land to farm, the men who resided in the Armenian villages were often absent from their families for months or even years at a time to earn a living elsewhere. Many were craftsmen or traders who ventured as far as Dikranagerd or Kharpert to find work.

Life was intolerable because the idle and thieving Kurds would happily break bread with Armenians in the morning, satiate themselves, then rob them at night.

Basically, these two villages, Srin and Baghin, were the Kurds' milch cows. The bandits sometimes even worked up the audacity to abduct beautiful Armenian women, an act that would usually result in bloodshed.

The Armenians were also as brave and courageous as the Kurds. But they could not continue to live and struggle like this until the first wave of emigration to America.

In all likelihood, my *hav*, unable to go on living under such conditions, and having lost everything (his home, his cattle, his property) fled the village at the age of 25 and settled in Til, marrying one of the daughters of the village's richest family, the Baghdoyans. My *hav* was well-liked by his in-laws. He lived and worked with them for some time. Later, with their help, he acquired his own hovel, but he was still considered poor because he was still his in-laws' ward and depended on them for his income. Having the personality unique to the people of the mountains, Hagop quickly earned the respect of his new neighbors.

This strong man would have four sons, all of whom would later be known for their courage.

Hagop worked tirelessly to ensure the well-being of his wife and four children. He was in the service of his in-laws' home, sometimes took the village herd to pasture, and occasionally worked for his fellow villagers. His children began growing up. During the summer harvest, his four sons would work under the searing sun in the dry fields, in bare feet, collecting the stalks of wheat left behind by the field workers. This work was called *hasgahavak* (*bashakh*). In Armenian villages, it was customary for each field hand doing the harvesting to have the sons of an indigent family doing this work for him. Such families, who didn't have their own fields and farms, were often also employed by their other neighbors to do field work. They were the *jilvelegs* – the landless.

Such was life. The patriarch of our clan worked as much as he could, while his sons Yeranos, Sarkis, Mgridich and Asadour, wearing their straws shoes, practiced *bashakh* to help the family eke out a living. Their mother, to save money, would send her sons to the field with only a loaf of *gulgul* or corn bread per day. Despite having been the daughter of a rich man, she never complained of having married a poor servant who had condemned her to a life of poverty and penury.

Naturally, she felt the pangs of her poverty when she sent her sons to work half-famished with nothing but dry bread. There were instances when the boys were forced to steal bread from their own mother. She thought of different ways to hide the bread from the boys. She would hide it in large jugs, thinking the boys could not get into them. But Sarkis could not tolerate hunger. He was determined to get the bread out of the jugs. But how? The jugs were deep, and the boys were still very small. Eventually, Sarkis found a long, thin pole, sharpened one end of it, and fished the bread out of the jug with it...

The children came of age in this atmosphere of destitution. Four healthy boys, a father, and a mother, all working together, economizing, until eventually, like others, they, too, had their own herd, land, cattle, home, etc. They bought orchards and grew vines. Until that day, nobody in the village of Til had owned their own property. All the lands had belonged to the begs, who had inherited them. Each beg or agha was the owner of arable lands and fields in seven, eight, or up to ten villages.

My great-grandfather, my *hav*, used who knows what clever trick or diplomatic sleight of hand to gain the right to purchase countless plots of land from the begs. He soon owned not only fields and land, but also a mill and a mine. He and his family acquired thousands of sheep and goats, but as they owned no pastures, they had trouble finding grazing lands for their animals.

As children, we were told that during the first years of the reign of Sultan Aziz, the ruler visited all the provinces, all the way to the east, to study local populations and conditions. On a terrible winter day, while visiting the nearby buried ruins of an ancient city, he reached the village of Til, in the southeast [*sic*, south-west] of Palou, about three hours from the city.

He reached the village with his retinue at night and knocked on the first door he came upon, which happened to belong to my ancestors. Until then, my family had been called Kasigian, which was my *hav*'s surname. My *hav* was already old by this time, with his four sons married and with their own large families. In the morning, when the Sultan awoke to continue his journey to Oshin, so much snow had fallen that it was impossible for him to set off. The road wound through the mountains and he would have been compelled to stay another day. But my *hav* thought of a way to help the Sultan – he arranged for his sons to bring the family's cattle out of the barns – sheep and goats by the thousands. With this huge herd plowing the snow ahead of him, and Sultan and his retinue reached Oshin safely. Oshin itself was completely Kurdish-populated and was located near Baghin and Srin. Unfortunately, by the time the Sultan reached Oshin, half of the family's sheep had been killed, suffocating in the snow.

Sultan Aziz wanted to know what he could do to compensate the family for this kindness and sacrifice. My *hav* and his sons were in desperate need of pastures for their cattle. The Sultan gladly heard their request and promised them a gift of vast pastures and a forest. Upon his return to Constantinople, he proved true to his word and issued an edict granting my family ownership of lands. From that day on, we became landowners.

Amazed by this unbelievable change in fortune, the Kasigians' fellow villagers began calling them *khral*, as they'd had the fortune to share a meal with a king and to honor him under their roof. This nickname stuck, and the Turks and Kurds began calling my family *khral oghlou* to express both mockery and tacit admiration (*khral* – king).

From that day on, our clan and the local Turkish chieftains were rivals. There was no end to the fights and arguments. The begs were not willing to accept the notion of an outsider competing against them while living under their protection. Hitherto, nobody had dared rise from the more modest classes and become their equal. All their subjects, Armenian or Kurdish, had lived as slaves, kept in a state of terror and dependence. The people had never breathed free, and whole generations had spent their lives groveling before their oppressors.

Our family threw the gauntlet to the ruling class. People had never known freedom and, as a result, thought of slavery almost as their duty. Each man thought of himself as his beg's *maraba*, or serf. If the beg did not grant them permission to work the fields, they would simply die of hunger. No ruling or exploiting class has ever treated its subjects as cruelly as the Turkish begs and aghas treated their serfs. The cup of patience had begun spilling, but there was no way for the people to rid themselves of their oppressors. There was no hope of external intervention. The people simply waited for the downfall of each sultan, hoping that the next despot would be comparatively kinder. Sultan Aziz was succeeded by Sultan Mourad, who reigned for barely six months, and left his subjects with the impression of being a mad drunkard.

Then came Sultan Abdul Hamid (1876). From the very first day of his reign, the horizon darkened. His policies and religious zealotry created a deep schism between the Empire's Christians and Muslims, leading to thirty years of continual bloodshed. Sultan Abdul Hamid should be remembered more as a bandit leader than a monarch. His sole objective was to wipe out Turkey's Christian population, especially the Armenians, who had become a thorn in his side. This beast, Hamid, was the idol of the empire's thieves, brigands, idlers, exploiters, and usurers. Guided with his anti-Armenian impulses, he armed the Kurds, the Yezidis, the Circassians, and the Tatars. He even solicited the friendship of the wandering gypsies. He awarded official honors to Kurdish sheikhs and begs, paid them generous sums, and encouraged their brutality.

Encouraged by the Sultan's attitudes and beliefs, the Turkish or Kurdish tribal chieftains increased their brutal treatment of Armenians. The tax collectors and gendarme officials robbed the Armenian villagers with impunity. They enjoyed the finer things in life while Armenian honor was trampled upon, and no Armenian dared raise a peep. They would take over the homes of Armenians for days or for weeks at a time. It was the duty of each villager to host and feed any government officials or gendarmes who asked for lodging. If the family did not have barley to give to their horses, they would have to buy some with their own money or find some other cereal that the horse would eat.

Whenever the tax collectors or gendarmes descended upon a house, the family would frantically hide away their beautiful brides or daughters. But the village Kurds would inform on them, and the Turks would torture or flog the man of the house, claiming that he owed two-three years of back taxes and had to pay the entire lump sum. If the man contradicted them, the beating intensified. Naturally, these actions were encouraged by the local begs or aghas, especially when the victim was someone against whom they held a grudge or someone who had challenged their authority. Needless to say, protests addressed to government officials were futile. It was the government itself which sanctioned these acts. Officials waited on the aghas and begs, hand and foot, licking their plates and groveling before them like dogs.

Just as the sheep, when pursued by foxes, resorts to the protection of the wolves, Armenians, despite knowing that the wolves were much more brutal, would go and complain to them, often coming to some kind of agreement that involved the payment of a bribe.

I'll give an example. Encouraged by the enactment of the deceptive Constitutional Reforms [1908],* Armenians in our village asked for permission to build a church and a school. The Turks thought, "Good, good... We'll see how this all ends..." The construction went ahead, but one night, they broke into both the church and school and completely robbed them, not even leaving a broom behind. Nightly robberies also targeted Armenian residents.

Sometimes, the families would be left with nothing but the ashes in their fireplaces. The thieves would literally clean out their homes and take everything that could possibly be carried away. Sometimes, the homeowner would be awake, but would pretend to be asleep, to ensure he didn't also forfeit his life. To whom could he complain? When the church and school were robbed, the people resorted to appealing to Teffiur Beg and Hashim Beg. My father, who was the village *melik* [village elder/leader], alongside the village council, implored the begs to launch an investigation as to how the wall of the church had been breached. I have not forgotten the words that Hashim Beg screamed into my father's face, "*Melik, daha nerdesin?*"

At the time, I didn't understand what *"daha nerdesin"* meant. I now do. He meant to say, "Melik, just wait and see what happens to you..."

When Armenians appealed to them and said, "Begs, we have to rely on your protection. Why won't you grants us what is rightfully ours? Why do bandits break down our doors, while the doors of the Kurds don't even have a dent on them, and nothing ever gets stolen from them?"

The retort was always ready, "Armenians! You Armenians! You are a headache! You thought that you could just sing *'yashasun hourriyet, adalet, mousavet'* [long live liberty, equality, fraternity] and everything would be forgotten? That you would save your skins? That you would owe nothing to your begs? How could you be so foolish and naïve? What kinds of glasses are you looking through? You idiots! You morons!"

And so, Armenians in both Upper Hayk and Lesser Hayk cowered in terror under the reign Sultan Hamid. No Armenian was truly the master of his own property, his honor, or his life. The Turks and Kurds lived off the

---

* This is a reference to the Ottoman Constitutional Revolution of 1908 which proclaimed the equality of all Ottoman subjects. The gains of the revolution were never consolidated and the Empire slid into dictatorship, war and genocide.

labor and wealth of Armenians, which was enough to sake the thirst of the nightly robbers, day-time thieves, and official oppressors. Meanwhile, Armenians were left in penury, shod in ragged footwear, nothing but *tan* [yoghurt drink] or *tanabour* [yoghurt soup] with a piece of oven bread on their table for every meal. The field workers worked twelve months a year. They sowed, planted, harvested, thrashed, and winnowed the grain, then stored it in the barns in large piles. The grain would await the local beg, sheikh, or *hafuz* who would press his stamp on all four sides of each bundle. It would then be left in the barns for days or weeks, until the beg or the supervisor came to weigh it. The landowner would send men to watch over the barns, and the government would sell a tenth of the grain to an individual (*shahna*), who would erect a booth somewhere close to the barns to oversee this entire operation. The villagers lived in terror of these men who had the job of fairly splitting the fruits of their labor. For the duration of the process, the "shahna" would become a burden on the villagers who were forced to provide for his keep. When the day of weighing the grain arrived, he would stand beside the landowner and the *kuzir* employed by the village, and he would call out the weights like a crier, melodiously. The scales would fill and empty... One, two, three...

The villagers first had to carry the beg or agha's grain to his granary, and then the village's own share would be split into a thousand portions. First came the supervisors of the fields (*khoroujis*), then the vineyard keepers, the orchard keepers, the *kuzir* [village steward], the bell-ringer, the priest, etc.... The last to get their "galamasd" were landless families, the widow, elderly, and orphans.

We did not mention how the landed aghas treated their marabas. In the fall, when the beg's or agha's vines had to be pruned, the villagers had to abandon their crops and go work *"sourkha"* for him. Neglecting their own fields, they would prune their overlord's vineyards. Then the *kuzir* would make the rounds and give out orders – each household had to provide one man to collect winder firewood in the mountains for the beg's household. Another day, the beg's hayloft might have collapsed would have to go into the forest and collect twigs and branches, use their own pack animals to transport them, and rebuild the hayloft on that very same day, etc. This was all free labor. There was no pay, not even a word of appreciation.

Even in the winter, the villagers had no rest. They were worked like dogs in every season.

Once the snows came and covered the mountains and valleys, the begs would wish to go hunting on horseback. As the partridges would fly off, the villagers would be sent into the undergrowth to chase them down. Late into the night, in the snow and blizzards, the exhausted, half-frozen men would finally return home, many later falling ill with rheumatism and other ailments.

The snow would cover the roofs of the homes like a thick blanket. The roof beams would creak under the weight. In the early morning, the villagers would first have to take turns cleaning the beg's roof. If it was the turn of an elderly woman, she would either have to pay someone to go in her stead, or rely on the kindness of a neighbor to voluntarily take her place.

But let us leave this alone. It is well-established history. Let us return to our story.

It was, as I have mentioned, that our family had the misfortune to rise to such a position and to accumulate such wealth.

My *hav*, Hagop, had died long ago. His four sons worked as hard as they could but could not match their father's achievements... They had no help...

It was a good opportunity for our village's monster of a beg to finally achieve his goal – to crush the Khralian family, whose larders and storerooms fed even the family's sworn enemies. Kurdish highwaymen and bandits would come from far up the mountains to beg us for grain. Then they would still steal our sheep...

The conflict between our family and the begs had been raging for a century already. Sometimes it had raged under the surface, causing great damage. Sometimes there had even been clashes in the fields or on the barn floor. Naturally, the begs themselves always avoided the fray and merely ordered their servants and Kurds to pick fights with our servants, fights that often resulted in bloodshed. Whenever our family raised the possibility of legal proceedings, the begs would claim that they had no idea what was happening, that they had been absent from the village when the fights occurred, etc.

But eventually, my grandfather's brother, Asadour, fell victim to their machinations.

One of our neighbors' daughter was abducted sometime in the 1870s by the begs in broad daylight. Nobody wanted to interfere. But Asadour was a brave, young man. He threw down his scythe and ran to Yeghsa, who was being dragged away by 15 armed Kurds. He was gasping for breath by the time he reached them. He grabbed Yeghsa in his arms and would not let go. The Kurds began striking him savagely, stabbing him all over his body with their daggers, but he would not loosen his grip. He was able to save Yeghsa, but by the time the girl's family and other villages arrived on the scene, he was severely injured and losing consciousness. Asadour initially recovered, but he never regained his strength and died soon thereafter.

After Asadour's death, the three Khralian brothers initially decided to emigrate, to leave their homes and everything else behind. But the begs did not allow them to leave. First, they threatened them, then begged them not to go to other begs and become a bone of contention between them. Let me add that the province of Palou was ruled by a few begs and amiras. The entire population of Palou was ruled by these despots who were sworn enemies of each other.

As our family was constantly involved in conflicts with the begs, we had trouble hiring servants. Many of our servants had been attacked by the beg's servants. This situation lasted until 1895, by which time, the luster was wearing off the Khralents home. The family were sick of fighting and were willing to submit. Then came the events of 1895.*

The Armenian nation went mad with grief and did not have the time to keep track of its lost lives, wealth and honor.

There was one bitter pill that Armenians could swallow to save their skin – converting to Islam. But only the beautiful girls were allowed to do so. That's what happened in our villages – a small number of girls, women, and youngsters were allowed to convert. Many Islamized Armenians still lived across the Empire in 1915.

Those who survived the massacres of 1895-1896 were condemned to destitution. Nothing was left to them. The Turks and marauding Kurds had taken everything. The schools were shut down and the churches

---

* This reference is to the Hamidian massacres between 1895-96 when Armenians were massacred across the Ottoman Empire. The number of victims have been estimated at over 100,000 Armenians.

desecrated, their golden censers and chalices already sold off, and their parchments, manuscripts, and chronicles burned in the village.

In that year, Teffiur Beg confiscated our family's wealth and seized our properties, leaving us with enough land for a large family to survive. The three brothers had been killed. Asadour was dead. The only one left was my grandfather, Yeranos.

My grandfather toiled day and night to send his precious son Arisdages to be educated at school. At that time, education was limited to lessons in Christian catechism. The village was so isolated from the outside world that sometime in 1912-1913, when we heard that a couple of Russians were in the area, a few 9-10 year-old friends and I snuck away and trekked to a village two hours away to see if these Russians were human beings just like us…

First Memories

During my childhood, our village had neither a church, nor a school. Everything had been razed to the ground in 1895. The villagers seemed to still be stuck in a horrifying nightmare. The generation of 1895, meaning our fathers, had virtually no education. A few of them were literate, having learned the Nareg and the Psalms. They were content with being able to read and write simple correspondence.

We were children. Incorrigible boys, growing up in the streets and fields. When spring came, we would wander the mountains and collect irises, or take the kids or lambs to the pastures. We would tie daisies together in golden chains. We would slice the stem of one daisy with our nail, then insert another daisy's stem into it, and so on. We would make long chains and hang them around the neck of our best calf or kid. We were knaves. The most repulsive curses heard on the streets were the crown jewels of our lexicons. When we got into fights with Turkish hoodlums, you should have seen the bloody faces we and they all got! When they tried to interrupt our games, we had no patience for them, and would immediately fight with them.

I will never forget one awful event, when I reaped the fruits of my mischief.

As one philosopher correctly observed, "Boys have no fear of the future because they don't have a past." Our fathers paid the price of our transgressions. They atoned for our innocent sins. When we beat up Turkish or Kurdish hoodlums in the fields or the mountains, our parents had to compensate for it by either paying off the other parents or ingratiating themselves to them. It didn't matter that we, too, were often bullied. Our fathers did not have the ability to protest or threaten. All they could do was beg the Turks not to let their sons hound us.

We were three children, terribly obsessed with destroying bird nests and taking their eggs, especially magpies' eggs. These birds would usually build their nests on the highest and thinnest branches of the mulberry trees. On one occasion, I climbed up the tree first, but I couldn't get all the way to the top. The youngest one of us, being nimbler, reached the very top, took six eggs from the nest, put them in his pockets, and started climbing down. The poor magpie, on the lower branches of the tree, was frantically squawking and screeching at us. Soon, another magpie joined, and they both began harassing us. We knew that they were the male and female who had built the nest. We held the eggs in our hands, taunting the birds. We were so obsessed with this pastime that we then left the village limits to find another nest and more eggs to steal.

On our way, we came across two Turkish hooligans, who wanted to steal our eggs from us. They were older than us and I was afraid at first, especially as one of the boys' father was a rabid dog. A progeny of Slekents Rumo. This boy asked Onnig to hand the eggs over, claiming we had taken them from his family's mulberry tree. Onnig was older than I, and I was older than Armenag. Onnig gave him one of the eggs, but the boys asked for the rest. Throughout this time, I was standing at some distance from the group, in an obsequious stance. I knew that Onnig was a coward and that he would hand the eggs over, but I had my hopes pinned on Armenag. As for me, I wasn't as much scared of the boys as I was of their parents, who were the worst of the worst. When Onnig finally relented and prepared to hand over the rest of the eggs, Armenag began trembling with rage. I, yellow with fear, watched him intently. Suddenly, he screamed at Onnig, "Hey! Don't give them anything! Run away!"

Armenag's words shook me out of my passivity. I suddenly felt a surge of courage. Right as Armenag called to Onnig, Rumo's son struck Onnig with a powerful blow. Armenag jumped into the fray, grabbed the Turk by the collar, and began punching him. Onnig ran away in tears. Meanwhile,

I, encouraged by Armenag's actions, ran up to help him. But the Turkish boys let Armenag go and ganged up on me. They thrashed me thoroughly while Armenag threw stones at them from a distance. Then, once they were done with me, they ran after Armenag. Eventually, I found myself alone. I went home in tears, but told no one of these events, dreading the consequences.

The next day, my uncle had tied our white horse in a corner of our garden to graze. He had instructed me to wait until noon, then to move the horse and tie it to something else. It was a very good-natured horse, and I loved riding it very much. But how could I get on its back? I thought of a way. I would leave the horse alongside the garden wall, and then scale the wall and jump onto the horse's back.

The horse kept grazing, and I remained buried in my thoughts. I dreamt of the revenge I would have on the Turkish boys for having beaten me up. Armenag had gained great stature in my eyes. I thought of him as an intrepid knight. Meanwhile, Onnig had been reduced to a pathetic, sniveling figure in my mind. Truly, the greatest of the seven pillars of life is COURAGE.

I was still lost in my thoughts when I was jolted back to reality by an unknown voice calling me in Kurdish. Though I wasn't fluent in Turkish or Kurdish, I certainly understood every curse in either language.

"Mu du mar day tonno… [I… your mother] Was it you who resisted us and fought back the other day? Were you the one?" And he began throwing stones at the horse. It was Rumo's son, this time with another friend of his. They started attacking the horse with sticks and stones. I couldn't dismount and held on to the horse's mane for dear life. The horse wasn't saddled, so it was all I could do to hang on. Eventually, the horse panicked and ran headlong into the trees and bushes. There was nobody I could call for help.

I don't know how long the horse ran around. Eventually, it bucked and threw me off its back. That's all I remember, nothing else. I lay on the ground, blood running down my face, my bones bruised. I was in that state when they took me home. For a whole month, I was in intense pain and delirium. I wasn't even able to tell my family what had happened to me.

First Memories

***

Our life of dissipation was to come to an end. We would no longer remain unkempt and uneducated. We would no longer pick fights with Turkish urchins.

A school was to be opened in our village, and a church was to be built.

They began building the church and school. All of us children helped with the work. With our little hands, we carried stone, wood, sand, and anything else needed by the builders.

I don't remember the end of the construction work, but eventually we found ourselves inside the classrooms, learning the Armenian alphabet. Our teacher was a kind man, who did everything he could to teach us how to read and write.

Our teacher was different from most others. We could see that the local Turks were not as satisfied with him as they had been with his predecessor, Boyajents Boghos. Even Boyajents Boghos, an elderly man, hated Minas, our teacher, even though the latter was his nephew. Minas, in his turn, despised his uncle.

We did not know why they disliked each other. Boghos and others like him lived in close accord with the Turkish and Kurdish begs, and, in contrast, avoided people like my father, Baghdoyents Ghazar, and our teacher. When they ran into the latter in the streets, they greeted them perfunctorily and quickly walked away. This phenomenon made an impression on our young minds. Even though Boghos and his friends had always been kind to us, we would flee from them. Something like fear had begun establishing itself in our souls.

But I do remember one thing very clearly – the Turks would sometimes joke that Khralents Dakes (Arsidages, my father), Ghazar, and Minas were "khart (fervent) giavours [infidel] and couldn't be good neighbors."

In subsequent years we discovered that these men who weren't deemed good neighbors of the Turks were men of a certain ideology. I won't go into specifics, dear reader. You can give whatever name you want to men of such ideas, whom neither I nor you understand.*

---

* The reference here is to Armenian revolutionaries who opposed the autocracy of Sultan Abdul Hamid II and advocated the equality of all Ottoman subjects.

[* * *]

As the proverb says, the fruit of the forbidden tree is sweet. I don't know how we had learned this song, *"Olan giavour, doghrou seoyle, Bankayı basan sen mi idin?"* [Hey, infidel, tell the truth, Were you one of the people who attacked the bank?]

"Khayur, efendim, iftira dır." [No sir, that is slander]

"Dasnuyergouken megu yes em, oukhd uradz em, chem user." [I'm one of the twelve, I've pledged, I will not tell].*

What was with this mixed Turkish and Armenian song that was forbidden? We were even strictly instructed to never sing it outside the home. I would be bursting, going mad, but I would not be able to belt it out. So many times I wanted to scream out "Olan Giavour," but an invisible hand always tied my tongue, and my voice died out in my throat. Some said that if the Turks heard anyone singing the song, they would hang them.

It was spring. The breeze blew gently, and the almond trees were in bloom. In the orchards, early in the morning, a hoopoe kept calling softly, "Hoo-hoo-hoo... Hoo-hoo-hoo..."

The house was deserted. They were probably all in the fields. Only my aunt was there, humming a sad song while churning butter. I knew the sounds of the churn and could tell when the butter was almost ready. The churn would start off making a *khesh-khesh-khoush* sound, but once the milk had almost turned to butter, it would make a more muffled *dzep-tep, dzep-tep* sound.

I was standing alone on the balcony or on the roof, lost in my thoughts.

I wondered what would happen if I suddenly belted out that forbidden song, *"Olan Giavour."* The murmur of the Euphrates flowing nearby and the song of the hoopoe would probably drown me out. I thought it over as I looked around. I could see nobody. Total tranquility. It was a good opportunity for me to sing loudly, *"Dasnuyergouken megu yes em, oukhd uradz em, chem user."* I saw that my aunt was busy emptying the churn. *Pu-*

---

* This is probably a children's reference to the Bank Ottoman incident, when Armenian revolutionaries took over the main offices of the Ottoman Bank in Constantinople to draw attention to the plight of Armenians following the Hamidian Massacres of 1895-96.

pu, pu-pu sang the hoopoe. I seized the chance, and I don't know how I sang it, or which stanzas I sang, but I did, then ran right to my aunt. My heart was racing, and I was expecting some type of catastrophe to befall me, as if I had committed a terrible crime. But nothing happened.

I had been relieved of that terrible pressure. I breathed a sigh of relief. My spirit seemed light, as if I had just been born again.

I had broken the chains of my slavery. It didn't matter that that was the only time I sang the song out loud. It was enough that I had rebelled once, and that I had broken the chains that tethered me. On that day, I understood why we were not free to sing, *"Olan giavour, doghrou seoyle, Serop Pashayu tanurmusun? – Khayr, effendim, iftira dur, iftira. Engerneren megn yes em, oukhd uradz em, chem user."*

Blessed be the memories of all those who took that oath and kept the secrets; those people who remained faithful to their oath and did not defile the memory of our martyred nation.

Persecution

Teffiur and Hashim Begs did not see us in a favorable light. The Armenians of the village were gradually improving their lot, their children full of energy and ambition. This aroused the begs' envy, and they soon launched a new campaign of persecution. Although they enjoyed complete impunity and could do as they wished, they had to find an excuse to shut down the school. The construction of the church and school had been sanctioned by them, and they didn't want to lose face. The village Armenians had prostrated themselves before him and had promised huge gifts (bribes) just to be allowed a little corner and build their modest church and school. But the begs could not be swayed. The poor villagers went back to their work and forgot about the school. But then a miracle happened to resolve the issue.

In the entire district of Palou, the two most powerful begs were Teffiur Beg of our village and Ibrahim and Riushdi Begs of Sakarat (two brothers who ruled with terror). These were ruthless, cruel, exploitative and parasitic men. They would pay some hungry Kurd a bag of grain and order him, just for their own entertainment, to kill this or that Armenian.

These two or three begs were sworn, dynastic enemies. Successive generations of their families had been battling for supremacy for years. They had accounts to settle for disputed fields and entire villages, and they could not come to an agreement. A great amount of blood had been shed on both sides.

In 1905-1906, the issue of the village of Giulishger reared its head once again (the graveyard of Giulishger is the setting of a painting by the late R. Zartarian).

The village of Giulishger, which was half-Armenian and half-Turkish, was a bone of contention between the rival begs. As spring approached, and the time came to plow the fields, the begs prepared their *ashirets* for a battle. The victor would win control of the village. In April, the *ashirets* began clashing. The local villagers were forced to shed their blood for their begs. Hundreds died on both sides. A detachment of troops was sent from Palou in an attempt to restore peace. The governor of Dikranagerd [Diyarbekir] was appraised of the situation (at the time, Palou was under the jurisdiction of the Dikranagerd governorship).

In the face of these reinforcements, the two begs surrendered and were taken away. They were exiled to Yetesia (Urfa) until their trial and were kept under guard.

Before the start of the trial, our beg sent a letter to our village and even sent his representatives with a separate letter to the *melik* (*res*) [leader] of our village, who was my father, instructing him to be ready to testify on his behalf. "If you promise to do everything to help me, I will give you permission to build the church and school you want."

The news caused an uproar in the village. It was time to seize the opportunity. The village council wrote back to the beg, promising to help him at any cost. And thus, we got our church and school. I don't know the details of the trial or how the issue between the two rival begs was resolved, or how much the villagers contributed to the outcome. All I remember is that both begs (Teffiur and Riushdi) were held in Yetesia for four years. Riushdi Beg's brother, Ibrahim, was not detained. Eventually, after four years of proceedings, our beg's rival won, and Teffiur Beg received a prison sentence.

When the court issued its verdict, Teffiur Beg went mad with rage. Foaming at the mouth like a rabid dog, he cursed the government authorities, his own religion, and his sultan. He loudly proclaimed that if he were not freed within three days, he would set fire to the government building and the entire city.

These were not idle threats. The Turkish government had long been convinced that these *derebeyi*s [regional chieftains], these vipers who had appointed themselves rulers, were a threat to the country. They realized that Teffiur Beg could easily carry out his threats. Under the guise of giving him a six-month reprieve from his sentence, the authorities sent him back home. Teffiur Beg returned to an extraordinary reception. All his subjects, all the *marabas* of his fields – in short, the population of seven to ten villages came out to welcome him back with trumpets, drums, and cheers. There was no counting the number of animals slaughtered. For a whole week, the people enjoyed a holiday, even though it was harvest time. Many joined the festivities and feasts only reluctantly.

Our village, too, had to join the crowds in welcoming Teffiur Beg. My father, however, did not go, nor did anyone else from our family, as the beg had no desire to acknowledge us. He was full of bitterness towards the Khralents clan.

During the four years that Teffiur Beg was confined, our village had been able to breathe freely. Of course, Hashim Beg was still there, but he was a young man, 28 or 30 years old. He did not have the authority that his uncle had, nor did he have the same reputation as a thief and murderer.

Taking advantage of this period of calm, my father had bought a few hundred pounds' worth of land from Kasum Agha. Hitherto, nobody in the village had the right to buy or own land, except for the few plots that our family and the Baghdoyents family already owned.

Upon his return from Yetesia, our beg was as truculent as ever. As soon as we heard that he had been released, we all felt a chill in the marrows of our bones. "May you go and never come back" had been the wish of thousands of human beings, but the curse had missed its mark.

Even we, the schoolboys, were infected by the prevailing sense of fear. And, in fact, soon enough, the beg's ruthless hand reached into our modest and unimposing school.

First, he ordered the church bell to be silenced, claiming that it disturbed his sleep and that his wife did not like it. So the belfry was silenced, the same belfry whose shrill bell had a history of multiple centuries, and whose peal was thought to be audible from two hours away. Its peal shook the mountains every evening as it marked the setting of the sun. The farmers and field hands, working in the fields, would hear it, straighten their backs, put away their scythes, thank the lord, and return to the village.

The belfry was the village clock, a necessity for the farmers, the pickers, barn hands, and the pious.

But alas, our beg silenced it. And God did not demand an explanation from him. From that day on, the village always seemed deserted and empty.

The beg had ordered the belfry to be silenced. So Anajents Khacho would not ring it. But the beg was far from satisfied. The school was still operating. He knew what the teachers taught and the direction in which they led the pupils. Armenian children had become a thorn in the beg's side.

One Monday, early in the morning, the beg's adviser, or rather his henchman, a large Turk with a fearsome face and a white beard, appeared at the school and demanded that the teacher hands over the son of Khralents Dakes and Armenag, the son of Nshan.

The presence of a Turk in our school was unsettling, especially the beg's right-hand man, who was seldom seen unless he was sent on an important errand… Something serious was brewing. The boys exchanged stunned glances. I don't know what he and the teacher talked about, but it was clear that he did not know the boys by sight, and eventually he left. We had no idea why he had come. After his departure, the teacher explained to us that the beg's wife had wanted to see the two of us because she claimed that on the previous Sunday, while playing outside, we had thrown a stone at her house and broken a window. The broken glass had supposedly injured her head.

Upon hearing this, I broke into tears. I had not been playing with the boys on that day, nor had I thrown any stone at the beg's house or broken any windows. At first, it was thought that some of the other boys may have committed this transgression, but once they were all questioned, it became clear that none of them were guilty – especially I, who was a particularly cowardly and melancholy child.

Although the Turk returned to his master empty-handed, we were certain that he would be back, especially as our teacher had only convinced him to leave the school by claiming that the two boys he'd been looking for were absent. I was afraid that we would be taken away and severely beaten. The fear of Turks, especially begs, was in my bones and in my veins. I could not fathom the possibility of there being kind Turks, and to this day, my opinion remains the same. I felt the lashes of supposedly "kind" and "compassionate" Turks on my own skin.

It was inevitable that we would be tracked down. The orders of the begs were imperatives, the orders of our grand *khanum* even more so. The teacher sent us home, hoping that they would forget all about it and wouldn't pursue us.

Less than two hours later, two boys came to our house to summon me. I broke into tears and refused to go, but the boys said that our teacher had sent word that I should feel safe and go with them. Eventually, the other "wanted" boy and I agreed to go with the Turks. When we were presented to the khanum, she smiled at first and called me over to her, *"Khral oghlou, bouraya gel."* I bowed and approached her. She patted me on the back and said, *"Aferin,* my boy, you're a smart one!" I was taken aback by her seemingly affable demeanor. Encouraged by this, I gained a little courage and began acting more like a schoolboy. After a few more questions, she asked, "What are you learning in school? Are you learning Turkish?" etc.

I answered her questions as well as I could, always remaining polite. I got the impression that she was satisfied with my answers. My fears had almost entirely faded away. It was now Armenag's turn. But instead of asking him the same kind of questions, the Turks threated him, *"Khunzur oghlou, giavour oghlou* [Son of a pig, son of an infidel], you're misbehaving, behave like your friend over here," etc.

There was no talk of broken glass, nor any sign that the khanum's head was injured. But she did slap Armenag across the face with a smile on hers. There was no other sign of anger on her part. Instead of pelting us with insults and curses, she gave us maternal advice and admonitions. After looking us over one last time, she dismissed us. We bowed and walked out.

We did not understand why she had wanted two young boys – two Armenian boys, to be specific – paraded before her. I did not understand what had happened, but part of me also wanted to go back and hear those words of praise from her again.

But my father was stricken with grief when I told him what had happened. It was as if he had heard news of a tragedy. I wondered why he was not happy that his son had been the object of praise. I wanted him to be happy for me. The more I told him of what had happened, the paler he became and the more he groaned.

It was strange. The atmosphere at home changed completely. It was as if we had been stricken by grief. I did not grasp what was happening. There were whispers among the family members.

One day, my father said, "Son, I'm going to send you to your maternal-uncle in Najaran. You can go to the school there."

"Why, father? Our school is better, and I don't want to be away from you. I don't want to leave my school. I won't go."

My protests were futile. They had been advised that this was the best course of action. They packed me off to Najaran, promising that we would occasionally visit each other.

I stayed in Najaran for some time. The school was no better than ours. In fact, it could be said that our village school was more modern. As I have mentioned, our teacher had revolutionary tendencies. He was progressive, and far from a religious zealot. But my teacher in Najaran, who was my father's own uncle, was notoriously pious and fervent. It was said that he "wouldn't tread on an ant," out of fear of committing a sin. Back in our village, we called each other *unger* [comrade] in the school, but here, we called each other *yeghpayr* [brother]. I tried to conform to this rule, but the term *yeghpayr* always sounded odd to me. The word *unger* sounded so much sweeter. I did not like this school at all, run entirely according to the wishes of Bedros Hrboyian. His mental capacities could not encompass anything beyond Christ, and his knowledge was limited to the Bible and the scriptures. He was very kind and pious, as I have already noted. He considered it a sin to lie, or even to discuss anything other than Christ or God. I remember how one day, at the church, we were reading the works of the prophet Jonah. Tears were rolling down his cheek as he repeated, "The prophet, in the whale's belly, screamed and beseeched, 'My Lord, My Lord!'" and his voice wavered as his sobs choked him.

There was no Protestant community in the area, and we couldn't think of another explanation for his extraordinary fervor.

He was renowned far and wide for his singing voice. Ultimately, the people would not leave him in peace, until he was appointed as the priest of the village of Turkhe (where he took the name Der [Father] Vahram).

Soon after my departure to Najaran, our village beg decided that he no longer wanted Minas to teach at the village school. Already, some of the villagers were grumbling, too. A conspiracy was hatched, and Minas was deprived of his position. In his place, they brought in a young man from outside – a youth with absolutely no experience.

After this decision, our village school gradually declined, eventually closing after five or six years. Teacher Minas paid the price of his actions in 1915. They came for him in the middle of the night, and his cries and screams still ring in my ears. In his own house, in front of his mother, wife, and children, they tortured him in the most terrible ways. That night, the elderly, women, children – our whole family was gathered inside our house, with death stalking us outside. We were crippled with terror, because at midnight, they would slaughter our teacher. He was to be kept detained by the beg for the duration of the day, so that he could tell him where he kept the money and guns that he supposedly had.

Our kind, virtuous teacher had neither guns, nor money. How could he produce it? They tortured him terribly in the "ghonakh" to force him to divulge his supposed secrets. Eventually, he couldn't take it anymore, and said, "Take me home, and I'll show you where it is. It's buried in the ground."

They took him back home at midnight. But how could he produce money that did not exist? They dug here, they dug there… The executioners dug everywhere, but found nothing. No money, no guns.

That's when the teacher truly ascended to martyrdom. "Oh you khunzur giavour! [infidel pig] You're lying to us!" The swords and *khanchals* [daggers] were unsheathed and plunged into his body. They whipped him terribly then applied hot irons to his flesh. All this was done in the presence of his elderly mother, his family, and his eight-year-old son.

I can't even go on describing these events. One could not imagine the screams, the wails, and the pain. I was so horrified that I desperately tried to cover my ears. The wails of his mother and his family reached the skies. We were on the other side of their wall, as they had gathered us all in the same building, and had already killed the men. The unfortunate teacher was not even given a proper grave. They threw his body into a minor valley near the village, and his corpse gradually melted away like fat under the hot sun. The begs' rabid dogs kept watch over the corpse, not allowing anyone to approach it.

May you rest in peace, dear teacher. You never had a grave. May my heart be your eternal resting place...

Just another memory...

Conscription and Exile

The world war came as a great shock to our land. Adult males, even the older men, were conscripted into the army. There was not a single household that wasn't stricken. There wasn't a single family that didn't have someone to mourn. The land became deserted. The wheat rotted in the barns. The authorities took all the grain from our granaries. Even the families of soldiers were despoiled, and their wives and children thrown into the streets. Oxen, cows, horses, donkeys, sheep... They even took away the eggs and chicken. They requisitioned clothing, beds, socks, gloves, and whatever else they could lay their hands on. On the front, they used Armenian soldiers as beasts of burden, making them carry supplies to the trenches.

December 1914. The parents and families of soldiers kept hoping for letters from the front. Ominous rumors began circulating. The county's Armenians sensed that a terrible catastrophe loomed. They dreaded the arrival of the spring.

In those terrible days, the begs decided that they could no longer tolerate the presence of Apoyents Atam in our village. Atam was fifty years old, with a powerful body and the temperament of a revolutionary. He was the one man who, in peacetime, had dared sue the begs for having seized his fields. A farmer's large family could not be fed without its own fields. As a result of the seizure of his fields, Atam had been forced to wander the land to earn a living. His absence from the village did not please the begs, either, as they knew that by traveling around, he would learn of the situation in the wider world and come back and inform his fellow villagers.

The begs prepared a note of protest. Nobody knew what it contained. They presented it to the villagers for their signature. Many signed without even reading it. My father, however, knew Turkish well and asked to be allowed to read the note before signing it.

They did not want him to read the note, but they had no choice. He saw that the note was addressed to the *kaymakam* [district governor] of Palou and accused Atam of being a *komitaji* [secret committee member] and of inciting the Armenian population against the Turkish authorities. On these grounds, they asked the governor to exile Atam from the village.

They had even forced Atam's brother, Apig, to sign the note. A man had signed his own brother's death warrant...

My father first protested, but then yielded to pressure and added his signature. Immediately afterwards, he gathered the village elders for a consultation. They decided to preempt the official decision by asking Atam to leave the village immediately, and to flee as far as possible, so that the gendarmes could not locate and arrest him.

The following night, Apo's house was surrounded. They searched every nook and cranny but could not find their quarry. The villagers were in an impossible situation. The gendarmes, brandishing the note that Atam's own compatriots had signed, kept beating the men, focusing particularly on Atam's brother. But Atam had been saved.

Months later, the entire land of Armenia would become a slaughterhouse, and the begs had already sealed Atam's fate. When he heard that the Armenians of our village had been deported, he crossed the mountains and valleys on foot, spending the nights in the lairs of wild beasts and the days hiding in reeds and ditches, surviving on wild grass and berries. Finally, one night, he reached his beloved native village, hungry for news of his family and children.

He knocked on his home's door, softly calling, "Apig! Hagop! Yeghsa! In-law! Harout!" But he received no reply.

Poor man. He did not know that the whole village had been emptied, and only the chirping of the crickets disturbed the deep silence that ruled the old Armenian houses.

Just as he knocked on the door, he was spotted by a group of Kurds who were purportedly out to hunt. This cruel twist of fate led to Atam being detained. The Kurds took him away, and after torturing him all night, killed him.

We saw Atam's corpse. His hair and beard had grown very long, unkempt and dirty like the hair of the dervishes of the deserts. His body was covered with blue welts.

***

My father and his fellow villagers had been arrested and taken to the beg's "ghonakh," where they were now awaiting their fate.

While they were still detained, the Armenian children of the village were scattered as servants among the local Muslim households, to be assimilated among Muslims.

One Kurd, who had been a servant in our home for a long time, and who had been raised on our bread and water, rushed to take me to his home.

That day, there were lots of Kurds stalking the streets of our village. They were all strangers, and were all armed with clubs and *najagh*s [hatchets]. Children as young as seven were walking around armed. There was lots of bustle. They kept telling the Armenians that "an amnesty had been issued," and that they had nothing to worry about. They opened their handkerchiefs before the men who had been arrested, hoping to receive some kind of payment or bribe for the *miuzhde* [good news]. Some of the Armenians, believing the Kurds, gave them whatever money they had in their pockets.

I came out of the Kurd's home to look for my father. I had only taken a few steps when several Turks began running after me to kill me.

Crying, I ran back into the Kurd's home.

The family admonished me not to go outside alone, warning that I would be killed if I did. They laid a few rags of Kurdish clothing before me so that I would not be recognized by the fanatics. I looked at the clothes and shivered. How could I defile my own appearance? How could I don the attire of my Kurdish enemies? When we took communion at church, we vowed to never sit at a table with even a Kurd's servant, or to eat from the same plate as a Kurd…

I refused to wear the clothes they had given me.

These awful people then sat me down and tried to convince me that I had to convert to Islam, that there would be no more Armenians left, only those who converted. But only children and beautiful brides and girls were offered the choice. The elderly, middle-aged, and young ones could not convert.

I rejected all of this out of hand. I understood nothing of what they said. My young spirit was crushed, but I remained steadfast and did not reach for the Kurdish clothing.

"Are you going to put these on or not?"

I said nothing.

The Kurd became angry. He dragged me to the door by the arm and pushed me into the street, screaming, "Go and die like a dog, 'khart giavour'! It's a sin to save dogs like you. Look at him! No taller than my arm and still acting up. Clearly, these [people] can never become Muslims!"

I wanted to see my father. I finally asked the Kurd to accompany me to the "ghonakh." My instinct told me that something would happen that night. I relented in tears. I put on the clothing he had given me, looked at myself, and was horrified. If just changing my clothes put me in such a state, what would happen when they Islamized me and sent me to the mosque?

The Kurd and I arrived at the "ghonakh." Sobbing, I ran into my father's arms. All the men were gathered in the barn and had no idea what was happening outside. When they saw my appearance, they were shocked.

My father was moved to tears. He kept wiping away his tears with his handkerchief. He held his head with both hands, lowered his head, and was speechless. Everyone around us was overwhelmed with emotions. They stared silently.

Every time my father looked up and saw me, he gasped, and wept like a child.

The Kurd, displeased with this scene, broke the silence, "Agha! Why are you crying? I'll take care of him like my own son. He won't want for anything. Don't worry about him. Be glad that I'm taking him in."

What could my father say? It was a question of life and death. They were taking his son from him while he was still alive. What could he say? Couldn't they have waited until he was dead?

He began to speak. His voice was different, as if it came from the other world. He was so befuddled that his words came out in fragments.

"Go, my son, go! You're still too young, what can I say? Your brother's even younger, take care of him wherever you find yourselves. Always keep your eye on him. Make sure you don't become destitute. Be smart. When you get older, make our family thrive. These storms shall pass. Just remember how your father died…"

Then he turned to the Kurd, "For the love of God, take care of my son. God is in heaven, and your *amanat* [mercy] on earth. May your bread and salt be blessed."

"Fine!" spat out the Kurd. "Don't worry about it!" and he pulled me by the arm.

I dragged my feet. I did not want to leave my father. I yearned for him so much, in some inexplicable way. It was as if I had never seen him, never lived under the same roof with him.

My mother had died three years earlier. I was orphaned from my mother, and now from my father.

He kissed me one last time and walked with us to the gate of the courtyard of the "ghonakh." My head hanging low, and my heart broken, I followed the Kurd to the street corner. My father was still watching me from the gate. I saw that he was wiping away his tears with his handkerchief and was waving good-bye to me. That was the last time I saw him. An endless chasm came between us. We would never see each other again.

After these events, I witnessed such atrocities that even after all these years, the mere memories send shivers down my spine.

With my own eyes, I saw how Turkish and Kurdish cowherds picked young maidens from the caravans and brutally raped them before tossing them aside. But even that did not satisfy these murderers.

The Turkish barbarian wanted to ruin, destroy and kill everything. They raped, looted, and destroyed without pity.

I heard the terrible screams of the victims at the hands of their executioners. I covered my ears as much as I could until the screams ended.

"Ayskan charik te moranan mer vortik,

Togh voghch ashkhar Hayoun garta nakhadink."

[If our children forget so much evil,

May the world curse the Armenian nation.]

I am still haunted by the memories…

In the field, near the spring, I saw some people in Turkish attire. They were sad, broken, and in despair. Their eyes were full of tears.

Who were they?

Their expressions were not those of other Turks. They were cowherds and ploughmen, who had no song and no smile. Their lips were sealed. They were struggling under the weight of their pain.

The same roads that had been plied by caravans of camels headed for Mesopotamia, India, and Persia now witnessed, for months on end, different caravans. Masses of Armenians. Youngsters, elderly, women and children. These caravans did not march to the gay clanking of the camels' bells, but to the deadly cracking of whips and the rattling of swords.

At one spot, someone with their intestines spilling out, crawled to another corpse next to it, dragging his intestines behind him like a rope. Who knows? It was perhaps his brother's or child's lifeless corpse, another victim of the ruthless murderers. But the dying man began gnawing on the corpse. Elsewhere, another injured man, driven crazy by thirst, dug into the dirt with his nails, trying to reach a fetid pool of stagnant water made undrinkable by the heat. The moans of the dying, the weeping and sobbing, the death-rattle of the wounded…

But someone had to survive to write the elegy of this exterminated race. Someone had to survive to praise the honor and dignity of our martyred mothers and sisters. Someone had to survive and shed a tear for the unburied dead, to echo the dying throes of the victims to the world…

We were the ones who miraculously survived. We lived so that each of us could repay our debt to our beloved departed. Who asked us to recognize that we owed this debt? Nobody! We were moved by a much higher power.

1915 was our calvary. It was the most fateful chapter in the history of Armenians, and the author of that chapter was the Turkish race.

Where did the endless lines of caravans go? Ask each stone, each bush they passed. They will tell you.

Who were the great witnesses of this bloodshed? The planets, the sun, the moon, and stars.

Who will sit in judgment of this monstrous, reprehensible injustice? History, straight and impartial.

There are parasites who unscrupulously put the blame for these evil events on those Armenians who sacrificed their lives for the liberation of Armenians. There are many such people…

Justice, where are you?

***

Below the village, near our mill, a pitiful mass of humans loitered. They were a small group of women, like sacks heaped on top of each other. An observer, from a distance, would be forgiven to think that it was a mass of black reeds that had sprouted on the road. But these reeds moved and swayed.

Right outside the mansion of the "ghonakh," saddled horses kept neighing and whinnying. A little later, armed police-gendarmes came out and jumped onto the saddles. They were communicating with the begs with gestures and laughter. Clearly, the mounted gendarmes were signaling something about that miserable heap of humanity.

These were the remaining Armenian women of our village, elderly and crippled, those not blessed with physical beauty (the attractive women had already been snapped up). They had been gathered there to join others of their gender who had left for the deserts of Der Zor and the flatlands of Dikranagerd, never to be seen again.

I retreated into myself, barely breathing. I curled up into a ball, trying to protect myself from the world. My stepmother and other relations were ready to leave, but I, under the terrible weight of my pain and fear, hid in the hollow of a rotted willow tree behind the mill. I heard a woman's blood-curdling scream from nearby, right behind the willow tree, on the stream. She was singing a eulogy over a dead corpse, like the ritual mourners of old. I raised my eyes and saw that she was Shoushan, the young wife of Baghdoyents Garabed.

She had brought her two-year old boy there, to drown him where the water was deep, because she would not have been able to keep up with the caravan with all three of her children.

If only she simply abandoned him and left… But how could she? Was that possible? She was a mother, after all, a mother! She would not be able to leave…

How can I describe this horrific scene? I, too, was an accomplice in the death of that innocent, angelic little boy.

I was young. I felt nothing at the time. The mother had grabbed the child's little hands and feet and held him underwater.

The child was suffering terribly. He was struggling and trembling. His mother was singing the song of death. When she saw me, she called out, "Sanoug! [Godson!]," we were related on the mother's side, "come hold him down so he drowns. I can't do it."

When I grabbed hold of the child, he was already half-dead, but he rolled in my hands, floated to the surface, and suffered more. At some point, he stopped moving underwater, and I thought he was dead. I called over his mother, who was weeping at some distance. We picked up our victim and dug a shallow grave to bury him, but then discovered he was still alive and moving.

The mother gave him to me so that I could finish the job.

Eventually, he died… He died… We drowned that beautiful, angelic little boy…

As I grew older, I felt the terrifying spirit of that child, who haunted and tortured me. I could never, ever erase those terrible scenes from my mind. That child's spirit still haunts me to this day. How can I free myself from this nightmare? Where can I go? Where I can I run?

Am I therefore a murderer? How can I atone for my acts?

The mother joined the caravan with her other two children. They went and joined the child who had been sacrificed. And I, the unfortunate, am still alive.

The things we witnessed in those three months… I watched countless caravans pass by with my dry and sunken eyes. We lived as cowherds in the fields, our appearance completely profaned. That cursed clothing almost seemed to irritate our bodies. Only those who have been orphaned and found themselves in the clutch of the Turks can understand the full meaning of what we write with no exaggeration. Our wounds are still deep and fresh, and we can not help being overcome by emotion and anger when we read about the *yeghern* of the recent past.

My personal calvary began the day I entered service in the Kurd's home. They used venomous language when addressing Armenians. They were filled with such hatred towards Armenians that they wanted the dead to be resurrected so that they could enjoy massacring, killing and destroying them again.

But there was a poor orphan at their disposal and it was much easier to concentrate their venom on that hapless Armenian. My daily allocation of food consisted of two loaves of *lavash* bread and the sour *torakh* of spoiled *tan* [yoghurt drink]. This was the only food I had all day.

It was summer. Fire rained down from the sky, and I ran barefoot after the cattle in the thorny stubble of the fields. I was unaccustomed to this lifestyle and my former life had not prepared me for such toil. Consequently, I had a very difficult time. I would cry all day until my eyes were swollen. My feet were swollen because they were covered in thorns. I had difficulty even walking.

When we would take the cattle to graze on the banks of the Euphrates at noon, my feet would burn on the hot sand, and I couldn't take it. I would be forced to skip across the sand until I reached the edge of the water.

There, I would hang my feet over the edge into the cool water, and would quietly think, gazing at the peaceful and turbid waters of the Euphrates. I would think of how in the universe everything has its ups and downs.

I marveled how the Euphrates, which raged like a mad monster in some areas, could here flow so calmly and pensively like a backwoods brook, gurgling and bubbling as it wound its way downstream. I tracked the waves, which rose and fell like the chest of a sick man lying in bed. I followed these waves like a spectator following a funeral procession, until two, three, four, and more disappeared from view…

I suffered much at the hands of my Kurdish agha. I used to think that living such a life was worse than death. I envied the martyrs who had passed on and were spared new tortures. We, on the other hand, were living martyrs. Was it worth living with such privations and pain?

One day, I was grazing the cattle in the stubble field. I was sitting, melancholy, and thinking… Even I didn't know what I was thinking…

Suddenly, my fiendish agha appeared, ran at me, and still out of breath, started slapping me. I couldn't run away, as the field was thorny, and my feet were swollen. He beat me to the ground. Then he started kicking me mercilessly, ignoring my pleas. He screamed at me, enraged, "*Khunzur giavour!* [Infidel pig!] You're taking my cattle to graze in dry fields like this? Now I know why their teats have been drying up!"

I was beaten in the same cavalier fashion countless times. He enjoyed seeing me whimper before him. The neighbors, seeing my state, would try to intervene, "Msdo, have pity on him. He's unfortunate, he's orphaned. After all, you ate their bread, he was the son of a large family. Why do you treat him like this?"

The monster was displeased with such talk and grumbled that he did not want meddling in his affairs, especially with such futile attempts to stir his conscience. He could never tolerate the notion of conscience, it made him uncomfortable.

When something happens in life, people call it either a miracle or luck.

That day, as I was being beaten by my agha, whimpering at his feet, Hashim Beg, the same man who had sucked the blood and extinguished the lives of thousands, happened to be returning from the city and saw the scene play out. He pulled his horse's reins and led it to the agha and me.

"Why are you beating this boy?"

"Beg, may I kiss your feet! He's been very disobedient. To this day, I haven't been able to convince him to convert to Islam. On the contrary, he constantly denigrates our faith. He curses… He's stubborn, doesn't want to learn Turkish… I've seen how he and the other Armenian boys get together and speak Armenian."

"You dog! What does this little whelp understand of Islam or Christianity? And are you such a good Muslim, *khunzur*? How many times do you pray every day? I know that you don't fast, and you don't observe the rites of Islam."

And then, he drove his horse on the Kurd, and giving him several lashes, instructed me to present myself at his "ghonakh" that same evening. As I remember these events, Shoppenhauer's words come to mind, "As the sheep graze happily in the meadow, the butcher determines the fate of the sheep without the latter's awareness." So, it is with people's fate.

So it was ironic that the same beg who had killed many Armenians, the very beg who had killed my own father, took pity on me and reprimanded my Kurdish agha for attacking me.

But he was only rescuing me from one hell to plunge me into another.

***

I had been saved from physical torment. But instead, I would endure terrible mental and moral agonies.

I was incapable of doing any work at the beg's "ghonakh." My position was still uncertain. What were we? Nothing. Just shadows, satisfied with some scraps of bread, like unwanted and scabby mutts. We could not expect any better. Would anything be left to us from the table of a hundred dogs?

Thousands of people visited the beg's "ghonakh." Some were criminals who were on the run and enjoyed the beg's protection, others had dishonored their families and were escaping retribution. Some were being sought for robbery and took refuge there. In their own "ghonakhs," these begs played the same role that Sultan Hamid played in Yildiz. The begs were Hamid's disciples. All the wealth of the Armenians was concentrated in their hands, and they created their own coteries of aghas, effendis, idlers, and bootlickers. A pack of dogs who whimpered before their masters – a lair of knaves.

From these men, I was to secure a piece of dry bread or a spoonful of soup to sate my hunger. Three times a day, they would sit in three rows to eat around a huge oriental "sini." Often, I was left hungry. I was morose, suffering, and there were no friendly faces around me. There were some Armenian boys older than I. They had changed all of their names. I thought that these boys' souls had also been transformed, just like their names and attire. They looked like strangers to me.

I wanted to escape as far as I could, to a deserted valley where I could be alone and cry my eyes out until my soul was at peace. Crying is so satisfying, if only one is able to cry… The pain in the heart can only be soothed with tears. Tears wash the unsettled soul.

Gradually, I adapted and conformed to my circumstances. Having no specific duties, I was used as a messenger, sent back and forth. Thanks to my young age, I was allowed access into the harem. I was a servant, sent for whatever was needed, relaying messages from the "divan" to the harem, etc.

Turkish women were not allowed to be in the presence of men over the age of 15.

When I first stepped into the harem, I immediately noticed the sad and grim faces of the women, silently engaged in their own work. They all looked at me with tears in their eyes. Their gazes sent a shiver down my spine. These were the eyes of Armenian women and young girls, and their presence shook me to the core. My thoughts were overwhelmed. I felt ashamed, as if their glances were saying, "Shame on you, aren't you Armenian? Can't you see that before your very eyes, we are being defiled, we are suffering? You, Armenian men, will share the pain that each of us feels. You defile our honor with your presence…"

I felt the eyes on me from every corner, pursuing me. Where could I flee? Where could I go? Was I guilty for surviving? Why hadn't the monsters killed me too? The skulls of so many Armenian children and youth had been crushed right below the village, in the Khandag Valley. Why would Armenian women and girls blame me? Was I a man? No. How old was I? 10? Perhaps 12? What could I have done?

I truly was only a young boy. I was not guilty for the fate that had befallen them. They had been kidnapped, raped, and were suffering to fulfill the whims of begs, aghas, and the entire Turkish race. I consoled myself with my young age and hoped that Armenian mothers and sisters would be forgiving in their judgment of me. After all, I was not there of my own volition, either.

The beg's two young sisters headed towards the other side of the fountain, giggling between themselves. They whispered to each other and then burst into giggles again. With their braided hair flowing down past their waists, adorned with gold and silver trinkets, they peremptorily sunk into the silk cushions that had been placed on oriental rugs.

They kept staring at me, then at the group of Armenian girls, and burst into laughter.

I finally realized what they were doing… I understood that they were ridiculing us. They wanted to kill whatever was left of our spirit with their mockery and hatred.

How could I stand this kind of pain?

One of the khanums called me over and showed me to the others, "Sofia! This one, too, is a giavour's son. He's young, so he's free to come into the harem. You know, he's very mischievous, clever… The son of a bitch… but he's a 'khart giavour.' Would you marry him? Hmm? You want him? You love him? He's one of your people. Don't mind the rags he's wearing, or his sunburnt face, or his dirty and bare feet… Don't worry about that hole in his shirt that you can see through… They'll fill it up with grass and it will be mended…"

They hit me over the head with a stick. I felt like someone had poured boiling water into my head and all the way down to my feet. I was shattered. My spirit was destroyed.

They were insulting and mocking my young pride, right in front of Armenian girls and women who were strangers to me. I did not know what world they were from. My manhood rebelled within me. My national pride had been trampled.

My vision was blurred with tears. I couldn't see. I wished I were deaf, too, so that I wouldn't have to listen to the insults of these little khanums.

Who were these beautiful Armenian girls and young women? How had they been brought there? Why did they have to witness my moment of shame? A voice called from the bottom of my soul, a rebellious and brave voice. I was about to lose control and attack like a wild animal, rip them into pieces, punish them for their insults, scream in their faces and have my revenge.

"You dogs! You whores! You scoundrels who bully powerless children!"

I wished I had been a thunderbolt and could have stricken them down.

"You thieves! Murderers! Looters! Who do you think is to blame for my nakedness, for my misery? Who's responsible?"

I was trembling with emotion. My sobs were stuck in my throat.

"Hey! Khunzur boy! You bastard! Why are you crying? We're trying to marry you off and you're giving us a hard time! You don't want Sofia? We'll give you someone else – Khadije, Ayishe, Emine…"

Who were these Emines, Khadijes, Ayishes? They were the Shoghagats, Sirarpis, and Dikranouhis whose spirits had been obliterated. Each of them had swum across a sea of pain deeper than any ocean.

They continued chirping and mocking me like evil goblins. The Armenian women, the prisoners of the harem, remained silent, with lowered heads. Naturally, one was thinking of her brother's corpse, the other was picturing her son's skull being crushed against rocks, and so on. And the beautiful Sofia?

She was the daughter of a wealthy family from Trabizon. She had lived in the Caucasus for some time. She had been educated there. Then she had returned to her native city, where she had become engaged to a young man, also from Trabizon, named Zaven. During the war, Zaven had served in the Turkish army as an officer. When Armenian soldiers were disarmed, he crossed to Tbilisi and remained there for some time. But his family wrote to him to return to organize his wedding. Zaven returned to Trabizon, but less than two months later, was deported. As for Sofia, she and her family were deported in the last caravan to leave the city.

Her real name was Shoghagat. Sofia was the name the Turks had given her, but she had chosen it when they had told her that they would change her name. After their deportation, she, her mother, and her sister had reached Palou safely. At night, the whole caravan was told to stop on the historic bridge of Palou – more than 800 deportees, all elderly, women, and children. Policemen armed with swords blocked the two sides of the bridge. Then, a mob of "bashu bozouks," previously notified, attacked the caravan.

Then the massacre began. They killed without pity, and without a single firearm. They used sickles, axes, daggers… Anything else they could find. Some jumped into the water, choosing to die in a less brutal manner. Mothers threw their children off the bridge, and then jumped into the abyss themselves, falling into the raging waters of the Euphrates. But the mob, with the help of the gendarmes, stopped their victims from jumping. They wanted the satisfaction of butchering them. The attractive young women and girls were abducted and raped a little further. Then they were viciously cut to pieces and thrown into the river.

Shoghagat's sister, Sirarpi, was also dragged away. She clung on to her mother and sister, refusing to go. But pleas and begging made no difference. They hit her over the head with the butt of a rifle and she lost consciousness. They dragged her away by the feet, and like many others, she was never returned.

That same night, the surviving members of the caravan resumed their journey. Each of them was thinking of loved ones, a brother, sister, husband, or father they had lost. With bleeding hearts, they kept walking.

Shoghagat and her mother did not know what happened to Sirarpi. Was she killed by the monsters, or was she spared because of her beauty to satiate their bestial desires?

At dawn, the caravan reached the foothills of our village, three hours' distance from Palou.

The Turks and Kurds of our village had gone to watch the caravan pass, hoping to lay their hands on a victim.

Hashim Beg's horse healer (*seyis*) saw the beautiful Shoghagat (later to become Sofia), was amazed by her beauty, and thought that his beg would be happy to receive her as a gift. The gendarmes accompanying the caravan were acquainted with our beg, as they often spent the nights in his estate when they returned from their murderous missions.

But Shoghagat pleaded that her mother should also be taken along with her. She tried and they survived. She kissed the feet of the horse-healer, Farugh, for not having separated her from her mother, for the love of God. She could simply not go on living if she lost her mother after losing her sister.

God had at least answered one of Shoghagat's prayers. Her mother was with her, also a hostage in the harem. There, they melted away like butter, crushed by the weight of their terrible losses and memories.

And those Turkish wenches, those whores, were amusing themselves by mocking this wounded, bleeding doe.

The bloody scenes she had witnessed on the bridge were still vivid in Sofia's mind. Her wounds were still bleeding.

Here, in this mansion, mother and daughter were forced to suffer in silence. They had paid a terrible price for their lives. They owed their lives to their tormentors.

The beg's two sisters were beautiful but they craved affirmation. These *"kiuchiuk khanums"* relished mocking us. And why not? Hunters enjoy toying with their quarry.

They would often ask me if I thought they were prettier than Sofia.

They were always satisfied and happy when I assured them, "Yes, you are much more attractive and beautiful."

How could Sofia remain beautiful after having been flogged all over her body? For long days and weeks, she had endured the cruel blows of the gendarmes, had tasted the bitterness of life down to its last dregs.

Sofia was taciturn. She suffered alone. Her secret pain destroyed her from within. With whom could she share it? And what good would it do to share?

But despite all this, a stubborn smile remained in her eyes, on her cheeks, and at the tips of her lips. Anyone she met would think that she was smiling just for them, that she was born to bless everyone she met with her smile.

But she suffered alone, and became more and more melancholy. Her silence, her cold indifference, and the accusations she silently cast at humanity made her presence unbearable to her tormentors. They thought that Sofia was exacting her revenge upon them with her sullen behavior.

One day, they confronted the poor girl in her mother's and my presence, "You whores! You tarts! They dragged you away from the gendarmes and brought you here, they rescued you, and all so you could act like this? If a fly fell off your face, it would fall to the ground in 40 pieces. What are you trying to say? Maybe you're more accustomed to consorting with gendarmes…"

Their bile was directed at the other hostages of the harem, as well.

Sofia's mother, Emosh (I do not remember her Armenian name), begged and pleaded with her, "My child, don't do this. You're inviting disaster. What's wrong? Why are you withering and fading away? Winter is coming, they'll throw us out, we'll be eaten by wild dogs…"

"Mother, it's better to die than to live like this," answered Sofia.

She could not bear her pain. No matter what she said, her mother could not get her to reveal why she suffered so intensely. She could guess that it was something awful, but Sofia insisted, "Oh, mother, I don't know what you mean. You say I should be happy, but I can't."

Her mother would try to console her, "These storms will pass, we'll be free again one day. We'll find Zaven and live happily."

She would often milk the cows with her mother in the cowshed, about 50 meters outside the "ghonakh." I was drawn to her instinctively and would chat with her. Occasionally, her demeanor of a wounded animal would crack and show signs of life, but she would immediately rein herself in.

"You're so lucky," she would say, "you're a boy. You have a different kind of spirit from ours. Our pain is different from yours. Our pain cannot be healed."

Back then, I couldn't understand why her pain was so different from mine. I was an orphaned boy, clad in rags, deprived of all life's pleasures, the ghost of my father still visible to me at every corner. There was no fear or deprivation that I had not experienced. I didn't even have shoes on my feet. I cut a pitiful, sunburnt figure. I spent my days chasing scraps from the meals of the beg's servants and lackeys. At least she had her mother with her. I had nobody to console me. She could see all that I had lost, but I couldn't reciprocate. My heart had turned to stone.

The other women in the harem had told Sofia about my family. With her own eyes, she could see our old home across the street, which, though in ruins, still rivaled the "ghonakh."

She could see that I was just a child and worthy of sympathy. I was a bird taken from its cage, an abandoned urchin. She saw me as her younger brother. To ease my pain, she would put her arms around my neck, or would rub my head with her soft hands. She would gaze deeply into my eyes, and I would breathe in her intoxicating fragrance.

She longed for everything she had left behind. She missed the Armenian language; she missed her betrothed. She yearned for his kind and warm kisses.

As a younger brother and one who shared her fate, she saw me as the vestige of the life she had once known.

How she wished to share her pain and yearning with someone she could trust… How she wished that she could kiss me as she had once kissed Zaven.

But her modesty as an Armenian maiden opened a chasm between us, and her lips would not kiss my brow.

Perhaps she had recognized the extent of my suffering and discovered that the Armenian spirit had not died within me. Outwardly, I looked like a Muslim, just like she did, but my spirit had not been altered. But alas! In those terrible days, we were even terrified of each other. We were afraid of opening up. How we wished that we could say one word in Armenian! But who would be brave enough to go first? Who would be the first to ask the other if his or her apostasy was genuine? What if the other turned out to be a true apostate? The result would be the Khandag Valley, the grave of the martyrs.

Sofia would carefully tiptoe around the subject of speaking Armenian, trying to catch me unawares and have me blurt out a word. But she herself didn't have the courage. She wouldn't dare.

And so, we were very close, and yet we were very far away. We shared our pain, but there was no communication between our hearts. We could feel the intimacy of our spirits, but could not confide in each other. There was a wall between us, a veil that separated us.

It was impossible to go on like this. We had to establish trust. We had to find a way to communicate in Armenian.

Finally, one evening, I got up the courage to ask her. She had come with her mother to milk the cows. (Her mother did most of the milking, she was only there to help, to watch the lambs, empty the buckets, etc.)

"What is your Armenian name?" I asked.

"…"

I shared my Armenian name with her. A faint smile appeared on her lips when I told her my name.

"What a nice name. Zaven is a nice name, too, don't you think?"

She still yearned for him. She worshipped that name. She always hoped, believed, and waited.

"And you, Sofia? You love that Armenian man?"

Her smile now reached her eyes. Her heart raced, and she couldn't speak.

She didn't need to speak. Her feelings were all too clearly articulated in her expression.

Sofia was well-educated. She knew the difference between moments of joy and of pain.

I wondered why she looked at a mere child like me with such affection.

Gradually, she began seeking out my presence. She wanted me to be near her so that she could be free to open her heart.

***

I didn't see Sofia again for some time...

I was terribly distraught. I could not share my pain with anyone. I was alone, and a shiver ran down my spine every time I thought of her.

The beg's mansion seemed claustrophobic. I had changed completely. I had survived terrible trauma. It had been eight months since I had lost my home and been spared from the claws of death. But my wounds were still fresh, and still bleeding.

I ran like a madman into the wilderness and the fields. I wanted to be as far away as possible. I wanted to find a place free of pain and no worries.

I stopped. I was right outside the ruins of our old house.

The walls had collapsed. The courtyard gate lay prostrate on the ground. I looked around... I wanted to walk inside... But I did not dare. The doors of the barn and hayloft were open. It was dark inside. I gazed into the darkness with unblinking eyes, like a spirit. No smoke had come out of the chimney for eight months.

Silence. As if the ghosts of the dead were silently circling me. Anyone would be terrified to enter. I looked in from the threshold and examined the interior. There was no movement anywhere. I was amazed by how much things had changed. Had these ruins been a living, breathing house just eight months earlier? Had life ever truly prospered here? Had children smiled here? Had brides and young girls, blushing modestly, gone about their domestic duties? Had the pater familias bestowed his kindly blessings upon his children and grandchildren?

Had mothers really sung lullabies to their children under this roof?

Had I really, years ago, said my first "ungha" with my stammering tongue in this abandoned and dilapidated tomb? Right across from the house, in the "keoshg," I had performed the Psalms for the first time, at the request of my grandfather and uncles, "*Yeranial e ayr, vor voch kna i khorhourts amparshdats...*"*

---

* "Blessed is the man that walketh not in the counsel of the wicked" Psalm 1:1

(The author with his family). Missak and Sara with their children, Adroushan, Arisdages and Shoghagat.

My heart almost burst from emotion. I stood alone, face-to-face with my pain.

***

Since Sophia's disappearance from the harem, her mother had been reduced to wailing and moaning, like a lioness who had lost her cub. But she didn't even have the strength to mourn, and her voice would not escape her lips. Her last source of comfort, her last crutch, Sophia, had been taken from her. She had forgotten the myriad of other losses she had suffered. She only thought of her daughter. She couldn't even grieve properly. She couldn't force herself to ask the Kurds where they had taken Sophia or why.

We kept seeing how Kurds would abduct Armenian girls or women, satisfy their bestial desires, and then kill them ruthlessly.

The same would happen to children and teenagers. Many were taken in by Kurdish families as servants and would work all summer in the fields and barns. But as soon as the winter arrived, and the work in the fields ended, feeding these Armenians became an unnecessary expense. Is it not a shame, they would say, to waste food on giavours? It had been a whole year [since the beginning of persecutions], but they continued to put people to the sword. We were living corpses who struggled day to day. Every day we survived was a bonus.

Emosh, Sofia's mother, was convinced that they had taken her daughter away and killed her. But there were two conflicting opinions among the women in the harem. One group, led by the beg's two sisters, claimed that Sofia was despised, that she was an ingrate, that she was lazy, that she had an unpleasant personality and wouldn't convert to Islam, that nobody had ever seen her smile. That despite their kindness, she had always remained gloomy and morose. They concluded that it was better for her to leave the "ghonakh." They claimed that Sofia had been sent to Mehmed Agha's house in Harpoung (a Kurdish village) to work as a maid.

On the other hand, the harem's Turkish wenches and the beg's jealous old consorts whispered that the beg had chosen Sofia as his main consort and had given her a special room. But they would not say which building she was in. They were either too scared to say, or didn't know. Sofia's disappearance remained a complete mystery.

Her mother, her ears at the ready, would listen to both groups. "Let her be alive," she would moan, "let her be behind a rock, not beneath it. There is hope for those behind the rock, not those beneath it."

The beg's younger sister, Ferida Khanum, was like a poisonous viper who would brandish her forked tongue at the other captives of the harem, "You senseless sons of Armenians, this mansion will soon be too small for you, too, just as it was for that whore of a girl. You'll be sent after her and will lie in the dirt under the lettuces. She got what she wished for…"

Her mockery contained new and painful revelations, which settled the debate. But there were other terrible rumors circulating among the Turkish women who had been sold for a piece of bread. They treated the Armenian women who shared their fate even worse than their owners.

It was now an open secret. We were convinced that Sofia had fallen victim to her matchless beauty, and that her womanly honor had been handed around. From the beg's carnal desire to that of the lowest agha, she was tortured and raped, until her blood was poisoned.

In fact, Sofia had never been chosen as Mehmed Agha's maid, though she had been taken out of the harem. She had not been taken to the home of Kurdish Mehmed Agha in Harpoung, but to the "ghonakh" of a Turkish beg between the villages of Turkhe and Alkhatian. Once, the beg at the "ghonakh" had been so powerful that people were terrified of even uttering his name. But his downfall had come swiftly. The last beg of the "ghonakh" had been Nejib Beg, who had gone bankrupt and was forced into penury, spending his life in the "ghonakhs" of other begs. He would eat the leftover food of the servants. As the son of a beg, regardless of his poverty, he refused to work.

These were the kinds of people who hung around our beg's "ghonakh." These men were willing to do anything for a piece of bread. They always devised different plots in dark corners. They sought beautiful girls everywhere in order to present them to the begs. They would simper before their masters like dogs and make obscene suggestions to peak the imagination of their masters. They would beg for orders to commit the worst of crimes in their names. They always believed that even if they were arrested, they would be released after a show trial, and that their begs would protect them from retribution. Even if they spent time in prison, it didn't matter. That would have been the greatest of services they could perform for their begs. They would always be rewarded.

Nejib Beg had no one. He was a 30-year-old bachelor. He was extremely ugly in appearance. Smallpox had ravaged his face, and his eyes were set in deep recesses in his face. The people had a saying, "If you were to plant seeds on Nejib Beg's face, they would be lost in the furrows." His "ghonakh" was located at a beauty spot, surrounded by flowers and fruits trees. It was a paradise but nobody lived there. The door was perpetually closed.

This was where Shoghagat (Sofia) was confined, because in the harem, in the presence of her mother, Nejib Beg could not treat her as he wished. So he had decided to move Sofia away from prying eyes. His "ghonakh" was barely 10 minutes outside our village, between Turkhe and Alkhatian. It sat on a hill, like a rider astride a horse. It was separated from the village by a high hill.

Months had passed, but they had not allowed the mother to see her daughter. Nor was there any news of Sofia.

In that isolated "ghonakh," there were many other Armenian women, some taken from the caravans and some locals, all chosen to serve as temporary consorts. When begs had their fill of these Armenians, they'd pass them on to subordinate begs or aghas, until the unfortunate girls were reduced to skin and bone or died of horrible diseases.

Sofia, too, drank the cup of suffering to its last dregs. Gradually, she faded away. Finally, unable to tolerate the physical and emotional suffering, she became a sickly, catatonic piece of rag, discarded in a dark corner of her room.

When will God punish the men guilty of such appalling crimes?

Did God not see what was happening? Did He not hear the groans and moans addressed to his throne in heaven?

Yes, he witnessed it all, but he remained silent. He felt powerless to smash the fangs of the Turk, or to break his arms.

It was a beautiful day in spring. The sun was aflame in the evening sky.

The beg's adjutant (*sakman*) called me over and asked me to go with him. He didn't tell me where he was taking me. I was overwhelmed by a terrible fear. My knees buckled and my face became ashen. This was a surprise. Why would Siusli Hasan, the beg's guard, need a young boy like me after dark. I knew the man. He was a monster who hated Armenians. He had killed so many children, youth, and women that he was known as *khasab* [butcher]. One winter day, all the toughs were together, comparing how many Armenians they had killed. Arif Agha of Anatots had killed 95. He claimed to have raped a six-year-old girl before torturing her to death. But Siusli Hasan bragged that he had "killed 122 Armenians, so I will get to *jennet* [paradise]." As a response, Arif Agha had made a vow, "May my mother be my wife if I don't get to 100."

I knew that anybody who went anywhere with this man forfeited his life. For him, killing Armenians was one of life's simple pleasures.

My blood had rushed to my heart from fear. I followed Hasan like a shadow. He was armed, with bandoliers crisscrossing his chest and his *khanjar* in his belt. We set out. We made our way through the trees and we took the road to Pshmujer. I seemed to be having an out-of-body experience. I felt like I was simply being dragged along. My feet would not move. I would think that I was running alongside Hasan, but I would only take a few steps and then stop. My ears were ringing. I did not know who I was. I could see death clearly, walking alongside me. Have you ever experienced that terrible feeling, when you see death walking alongside you, and you feel its presence?

Hasan's voice called me back to reality, *"Oulan khunzur giavour, yiuriu bakalum, nichin dourdoun?"* [Hey, infidel pig. Walk along now, why have you stopped?]

But I thought I was running like the wind. Had I really stopped?

I had seen thousands of deaths, but I had never been so terrified. A year had passed, and I thought death had forgotten about me and had moved along.

We crossed the calm fields, still within the village borders, then walked up the mountain – victim and executioner walking together. The full moon illuminated our path ahead. I only had my shadow as a consolation, my inseparable companion, and the sound of my footsteps echoing back from the denuded flanks of the mountain and muffling the sound of my heartbeat. I did not want my executioner to hear my heart racing.

We reached the summit of the mountain. I looked back and saw the village, sitting quietly in the fields, as if in deep thought. Everything looked bleak to me. It was spring, and the green leaves and shooting boughs of the trees were grappling with each other, trying to settle into their final positions. How sweet was the village in this season with its greenery and thick canopy! But an ominous, cold gale of death blew and seeped into my soul. The trees looked like black-clad hangmen to me. In the moonlight, the cold barrel of Hasan's Mosin rifle gleamed as it hung down his back. I did not dare look at this implement of death. I averted my gaze.

Once we started going downhill, I didn't need to make an effort to walk. It felt like I had been launched from a cannon. I just wanted it to end quickly. I had lived for a whole year on borrowed time. I had been fortunate. That's what I told myself.

We reached a neat and handsome house, which was Nejib Agha's "ghonakh." We went upstairs and after walking down a few hallways, we walked into a room. I saw that someone lay in a modest bed. A pale lamp burned above the headboard. When Hasan approached the bed, the person in it, feeling a little exposed, pulled up the blanket and covered herself. I could only see a head. Hasan asked roughly, *"Kuz! Nasul oldoun? Seoyle bakalum!"* [Girl! How are you? Tell me!]

The girl looked up and answered with a weak voice, "Thank you, I'm fine."

It was Sofia, the beautiful Shoghagat. She had melted away like wax. She was like a yellow, autumn leaf, waiting for the slightest breeze to blow her away. Oh, how she had changed...

I had not seen her for several months. My heart almost burst from yearning, as if she were my own sister. There were no Armenians around, just a few of us orphans scattered around the land. That's why we doted on each other so much.

Sofia did not even dare raise her eyes to see who had come in alongside Hasan. We were not able to speak, but I could see how much she had changed. I was in shock.

I knew that she, too, missed me, especially as I came bringing news of her mother. I had so many questions to ask and so much to say...

We were able to speak with our hearts. *"What one friend feels, the other feels as well. Don't say that's impossible, there's always a way between two hearts."*

Yes, our hearts had the ability to communicate, even if we had to remain mute and our tongues were tied.

Beside Sofia, I noticed what looked like a bundle of rags. When I glanced towards it, Sofia looked down like a sinner caught in the act and mumbled something to herself. She seemed to be overwhelmed with shame.

The guard kept interrogating her, "Do you want us to send your mother here to you? The khanums don't want you back in the "ghonakh." We can send her to care for you."

They were determined to get rid of her mother, too. They were only keeping her mother to satisfy Sofia. Now that Sofia had no value for them and was to be discarded. Her mother was disposable, too. There were lots of hungry Kurdish women they could pay to milk the cows and run other errands.

Sofia, her head buried beneath her blanket, silently wept. And the tears filled her heart, just as her pain gnawed on her core.

Hasan went on interrogating her for another few minutes, trying to evaluate her health. He always spoke like a brute to me when he gave me orders, or at least that's how I felt because I lived in terror of him.

"Pick up that bundle and follow me!" he commanded.

I immediately obeyed. When I picked up the bundle, I wasn't very careful with it, and from its folds fell a red LUMP OF FLESH.

I understood what had happened. It was the fruit of Sofia's ordeals. The child of her enemy…

Sofia continued weeping. She never, ever looked in my direction. She felt guilty and ashamed, even though she, too, was only a victim.

Perhaps it hurt her even more to know that her pain had been witnessed by a compatriot, someone who shared her fate, and someone of the male sex.

I didn't know whether she'd had a miscarriage, or they simply didn't want to have a baby and had strangled or killed the illegitimate child by leaving it to its own devices.

But none of that interested me. Sofia's tears crushed my heart and unsettled my soul.

We picked up that LUMP OF FLESH and the beg's *sakman* and I dug a hole in one corner of the courtyard and buried the remains, as well as Sofia's heart.

Then we returned to our village. I was no longer terrified and no longer felt that terrible dread of death. But the sad image of Sofia would not leave me in peace.

My conscience tortured me because I could not do anything to help or console Sofia.

We saw each other again months later. She looked more miserable and more pitiful. She seemed to thirst for sympathy. But I, with tearful eyes, suppressed my feelings and remained silent. I could say nothing of all this until today, when I put pen to paper.

***

Sofia's mother, Emosh, was sent to look after her daughter, who had been sent to the village from Nejib Bey's "ghonakh." Sofia suffered in a dark corner of the Boyajents' home, wrapped in several layers of covers. With each day, her condition deteriorated. She and her mother were poor, they had no food. They were left to their own devices. Her mother would beg for food from neighbors and friends, and would feed it to her sick child. But Sofia was already on the verge of death. She was sometimes in delirium. In the evenings, I would take some of my daily ration of bread to Emosh. When I took the beg's calves and *bukers* [juvenile oxen] to the pastures, in the spring, I would supplement my daily meal with mushrooms, greens, garlic, leeks, and whatever else I could scavenge. My greatest desire was to be of help to Aunt Emosh and Sofia.

I had no awareness of what I was doing, but my feet always led me back to the Boyajents' home. I knew that I had been Armenian once. That Emosh and Sofia, too, had been Armenian. Of course, our elders and ancestors must have been Armenian, too.

But if I were Armenian, how come I couldn't speak Armenian? How come my name was Kadir, and not M... Emosh and Sofia, too, had forgotten their native language. Nobody wanted to befriend the hapless mother and her sick child. They were afraid that Sofia's disease was contagious.

It was my people's blood that guided my steps.

I did not stop visiting and shedding tears for Sofia until the day she died, until the very end.

Sofia died. After suffering for so long, her entire body had become swollen and discolored. She was poisoned… And it was that poison that killed her…

We dug her grave in a deserted valley, under an almond tree, beside which flowed a small brook.

I was overwhelmed with grief. I picked wildflowers in lieu of a wreath and scattered them on Sofia's grave. I don't know if I also shed a tear… Seventeen years have passed since that day. Her mother shed the last of her tears and walked away, to tell the world of her pain…

I visited the grave every day, but never saw her mother there. It was my pilgrimage site. I would gaze at it for hours and hours, and sweet memories would rush back to my mind. A few tears would flow down my cheeks. I felt keenly that I was a forlorn orphan, and that there was a huge emptiness in my soul.

From 1915 to 1918, the entire Armenian nation was put to the sword. For three years, Armenian blood flowed like a river. Even when the massacres ceased in the large cities, they continued unabated in the provinces. The Armenian women, who had been forced to convert and taken into harems, disappeared for known or unknown reasons. The same fate befell Armenian children, teens, and youth. They were killed when they got older, as the Turks feared their revenge. Those who survived continued to live as Muslims, scattered across the country. But then, the Russians' westward advance sealed their fate. They were killed because the Turks knew that if they were left alive, they would join the Russians and rise up against them.

But then, suddenly, good tidings reached us. The stork soared from mountain to mountain, from valley to valley, towards the ruins of western Armenia, heralding, "Armenia is free! The independent Republic of Armenia!"

The American Relief Fund [Near East Relief Fund] was everywhere. Wherever this organization had an office, Armenian remnants who had escaped the Turkish sword flocked to it. Many had been through hell. Traumatized Armenian mothers emerged from the deserts of Der Zor, many having buried most of their loved ones in the sands. Some had given up their children to the Arabs or Kurds, and in return had received the enemy's brand of disgrace on their foreheads or various parts of their bodies – brands that would never wash off.

The survivors told unimaginable stories of deaths, reopening wounds that had just begun to close.

News of Armenia's liberation finally reached the household of our local despot, Hashim Beg, where I was still languishing in servitude. I had still never left my birthplace, the village of Til. Aside from me, there were only a few other Islamized Armenian boys and Islamized women who had been carried away as wives. They had almost forgotten their native tongue and had resigned themselves to their fate. We were cut off from the world. We knew nothing of global events. Occasionally, Armenian travelers, returning from Kharpert, would tell us that peace had been restored, that they were free, that they spoke Armenian freely, that there were orphanages, and that Americans had come to liberate Armenian boys and women from the Turks, etc.… The Turks and the begs, too, told us that there was now an "Ermenistan" and that Antranig would be our king.

I was fascinated and excited by this news. I became a new person. I wanted to go and see this new Armenia as soon as possible, to have my freedom, to have my Armenian name back, to speak Armenian again… I had lived so long without my real name that sometimes I would suspect I had never borne it. It sounded so sweet…

I decided to run away, no matter what. But I had never left my native village and did not know the roads. I had to cover a distance of 12 hours to get from Til to the city of Kharpert. It seemed like an impossible task, but the desire for freedom can overcome all obstacles.

It was an autumn day. The trees were stripped of their beauty. In the autumn, misery seeps into the souls of the wretched.

I could not sleep at night. My cot was in the corner of the sheep pen, where I slept on a dirty and discolored mattress using an old, ragged blanket, whether it was winter or summer.

It was Friday. After supper, I left the table, but instead of walking into the sheep pen, I found myself headed for the vineyard. For a few minutes, I walked around the vineyard in the moonlight. My mind was full of thoughts. Should I escape, or should I not? I was still thinking this over when I reached the little depression where Sofia's grave was. I walked over to it and saw that the grave had been desecrated. There was almost no trace of it. For a few moments, I stood there, before her grave, and sobbed uncontrollably. Then, with my soul unburdened, I turned to the west and walked towards the light, towards a new dawn. I was now one of the thousands of Armenian orphans who escaped hell.

A Page from the Bloody Year of 1915

The spring of 1915 was unlike any other.

That year, the Euphrates seemed enraged. It was the month of May. The turbid river would overflow its banks, seething and frothing as it wound its way around the fields. It clawed at the land, ripping and dragging away whole chunks of earth, roaring and smoldering as it raged like a wild beast. And like a spiteful beast, it would occasionally change course and flood whole fields until it settled down again.

For the village cowherds, it was a fun time. They went to the river and tested their strength against its powerful currents. They eventually crossed the river and came ashore on an island, overgrown with tamarisk shrubs and bamboo canes giving the appearance of a forest. The boys made a search of this islet or peninsula, wondering what new wonders and miracles the angry Euphrates brought them every year.

The cowherds returned. They had found two mysterious corpses, both bearded, swollen, and with heads the size of domes. The more rational among them established that the bodies were still fresh. Many insisted that they must have been priests. That was because in the east, more correctly, among the people of Upper and Lesser Hayk (Armenia), only priests wore beards. The guesses kept coming. Some were sure that the bodies were those of deserters from the army who had been executed. At the time, by law, those who deserted or absconded from the army three times were shot. Eventually, these corpses became part of legend, as well as a great puzzle.

If the Euphrates could have spoken and told us what was happening in the dark, the events that later befell us would not have been so catastrophic.

The corpses of the Euphrates had not yet been forgotten when we started spotting corpses on roads and mountain paths, as well as in valleys. Nobody could make sense of them. A terrible fear began growing in our minds. People dreaded a looming disaster and lived in anticipation of the coming nightmare.

The land of Armenia was writhing in pain. There were whispers that Armenian soldiers were being disarmed and sent away from the front and placed in labor battalions (*amele tabour*s), which were a recent creation. The Armenians who had hitherto so unctuously served the Turks had suddenly become dangerous and disloyal elements. There was no longer any trust between Armenians and Turks, and a growing divide separated them. The Turks, whose livelihood depended on the Armenians, suddenly looked askance upon their Armenian neighbors. Their relations were gradually breaking down.

The Turks created new provocations and unrest. They accused Armenians of supposedly contributing to the rapid Russian advance, and biding their time for an opportunity to rise up against the Turkish government.

Fanatical leaders and idiotic officials in order to provoke the Turkish masses were spreading a thousand and one fabricated stories, claiming that Armenian *fedayee*s and *komitaji*s were secretly in contact with Russia, sending letters, so well-hidden between the shoes and hoofs of horses, that neither snow nor rain could damage them. It was also said that Armenians were placing messages in underground pipes and sending secret notes and correspondence to inform Russia to facilitate their advance.

We wondered where these falsehoods were coming from. They announced that the Armenians of Van and Moush had rebelled, a Turkish beg was killed some place, a Major was killed elsewhere, etc.... The poor Armenians could not fathom the true purpose of such ploys.

We knew nothing of the outside world, we were cut off from it. Where would the poor peasants get information? How would they know what was happening far and wide? Who knew? Travel had become dangerous for Armenians. People lived under very difficult conditions and knew nothing of what lay beyond their immediate horizons. The world beyond was more of a legend than reality.

Armenians were completely disarmed. They weren't even allowed to keep dull or useless pocketknives. The confiscation of weapons became a campaign of persecution. Many people were mistreated and tortured to death. History seems to have forgotten these events.

Armenians spent their days trembling in fear and retreated even further into their own shell. Many lost their desire to work. Their fear grew by the day because they instinctively knew that something terrible was coming. The memories of the 1895 massacres were still fresh in the minds of many people. That catastrophic date was a model embedded in people's memory.

We could smell the gunpowder in the air already... And our little village, which had no more than 25 households, was completely disarmed. All of the influential Hashim and Teffiur begs of our village and the Palou region, who were the owners, lords and masters of the entire province, as well as all other well-known leaders, assumed the responsibility of collecting weapons.

Not that there was any trace of the central authorities in Palou. The heads of a few tribes (*ashirets*) ruled the people, both Turkish and Armenian. A single beg controlled 7, 8, 10, up to 20 villages. The village lands all belonged to them, and the villagers had no rights. They were merely his *maraba*s (serfs). They cultivated the land and harvested the crops, paying the government a tenth (*ashar*) of the harvest, and splitting the rest with their begs.

And thus, Hashim and Teffiur Begs (who were a paternal-uncle and nephew) got to work and ordered that a certain quantity of weaponry be handed over. They knew who owned weapons and how many. Even when people didn't actually own any weapons, as the begs knew well, they were forced to produced them. The begs had two goals and wished to kill two birds with one stone – first, they wanted to collect the weapons from the people in order to ingratiate themselves with the government. Second, this was an opportunity to extract bribes. When their victims were threatened, the latter would be forced to offer bribes to end their suffering.

Therefore, bribes were offered, in the form of "presents," to lessen the suffering.

But they also had another goal, much more insidious and deep-seated. The begs had been nursing grudges against certain Armenians. The disarming of Armenians gave them the opportunity to pour their venom and settle old scores. My father, who was a prominent man and the village *melik* (*res* or leader), had been a rival to the begs for quite some time. If not half, then at least more than a quarter of the village belonged to us. The

Khralian family and the begs were always embroiled in lawsuits over disputed lands.

For this reason, despite the fact that we had already surrendered whatever weapons we had, they were demanding more imaginary weapons. They claimed that the Khralians had a gun that could be dismantled with keys, bullets which were the size of crows' eggs and did not make a noise when they exploded and released poison into the atmosphere, etc.

My family members were shocked by these accusations. They did not know what to do. It was a delicate time, the sword of Damocles hung over the head of the Armenian nation. We had to resign to our fate. I was young, and I don't remember all the details of how my father and the begs came to an agreement, or what happened to that legendary gun that we were supposed to have had.

Other than the Khralian family, Ghazar Baghdoyents had also become a thorn in the begs' side. When the Ottoman Constitution was supposedly reinstated [1908], the Armenians of the Empire breathed a sigh of relief. From that day on, the villagers decided that they would no longer provide free labor for the begs as they had done for centuries.

This had enraged the begs who wanted revenge. Ghazar had been one of the original rebels. He had always been brave, rebellious, and truculent, and had always scorned the authority of the begs. They had even tried to kill him during peacetime but had failed. It was said that the begs had promised a Kurd two "*charegs*" [sacks] of corn and a horse in exchange for Ghazar's head. It was only after the *Medz Yeghern* (Armenian Genocide) that the bloodthirsty monsters admitted to this.

Ghazar had already handed the weapons he owned to the begs. But he had been summoned again to surrender a six-shooter. Ghazar did not mince his words. In the presence of the begs, he threw down the gauntlet, "I have no other weapon. If you want to kill me, go ahead and kill me."

His fellow villagers were shocked that Ghazar could not restrain himself during those dark days and was inviting trouble. Those hapless Armenians thought that if they just obeyed like sheep, they would be spared.

***

There was chaos, furtive whispers, great hustle and bustle among the Turks. The neighboring village of Turkhe, only half an hour from Til, was massacred. The Turks fell upon them with swords, clubs and daggers to plunder, kill and destroy. We could hear the gunshots clearly. The sounds of weeping women and screaming children reached our ears. The ploughmen, abandoned their oxen and returned home. We, the children, who had been in the fields with the cows, quickly drove the cattle back to the village and hid in fear until nightfall. Even the cattle seemed to be fearing for their lives.

The animals were pointing their snouts upwards and sniffing while the cows kept bellowing. We were in shock and did not want to believe that there could be such killings in broad daylight.

We then saw a horde of people coming with their plunder and loot. They were all Turks and Kurds whom we recognized. There was no time to waste. I drove the cattle into the barn quickly and went upstairs. My father and uncle were sitting, distressed. We were all expecting to be killed. Slowly, the sun sank behind Mount Masdar. The twilight died away and darkness descended.

Our blood was running cold in our veins. We felt an inexplicable shiver, as if our teeth were chattering from the cold. We were cold from head to toe. A deathly silence descended upon the village. It was as if the Grim Reaper was flying overhead.

Nobody said a word. We sought solace in the sound of each other's breath.

My father opened his mouth to speak… But what could he say? What were we to do? Where could we go? The beg or a Kurdish neighbor for protection? Just as he was about to speak, we heard a terrible din from outside. This was followed by thousands of rifle shots. The village was encircled. The begs themselves had organized the assault. They had wanted to take the village by surprise with a mob of *bashu bozouks* [irregular forces] so that nobody would escape. The same plan was implemented in other Armenian villages under their subjection. They had tricked and gathered all men, telling them none should escape, otherwise they would be captured and killed without mercy. Clearly, this was a tactic to gather all their victims in one place, like a flock of sheep, and then kill them without any danger from surviving escapees. The poor Armenians truly believed that they would receive the protection of their begs, since they were the latter's "marabas."

This was their plan for our village, too. When they surprised the village by surrounding it, all young men tried to escaped, leaving behind their families and children. Some broke through the encirclement and escaped into the mountains and wilderness.

The attackers, seeing that people were fleeing, called out to them like town criers:

"Don't run away! Go to your beg's 'ghonakh!' They will protect you. The village is surrounded by unknown Kurds who do not know our village and want to plunder. But we convinced them to go away. You must take shelter in the 'ghonakh' tonight."

The children and women came out into the streets, already mourning and weeping. Some sought shelter in the homes of Kurdish neighbors, but the doors were locked. And so, every Armenian in the village abandoned their home and properties and scattered. The begs and their supporters patrolled the streets all night, supposedly protecting the Armenians. When the Armenians abandoned their homes, some sheltered in Kurdish houses, others at the "ghonakh," while those who had no faith escaped. Meanwhile, the begs plundered the village and divided up the loot. None of us had any idea of what was going on. We did not sleep that night.

We spent that night in a Kurd's home, but my father and uncle went to the "ghonakh." Another uncle fled to the fields. In the morning, we heard that he (Vartan) had been killed in the blackberry bushes, alongside Apoyents Apig and another person. Some who had fled returned and gave themselves up.

They waited around another week for those who had fled to the mountains to return. All the men had been gathered in the horse stables, awaiting their fate. All the women and children were gathered at the Toroyents house, like sheep in a pen, waiting. They had supposedly made these arrangements to protect us. At some point, when they realized that the only missing men were Baghdoyents Ghazar and Apoyents Atam, they began searching for them, hiding in wait by roadsides.

They knew full-well that Ghazar would not return. He had appeared a few times, like a ghost, around the beg's mansion. They had chased him, but he had vanished into thin air. Some people had even seen him behind the "ghonakh," in the valley, smoking a cigar. He had become a legend. According to rumors, he intended to kill Hashim Beg, kidnap his sisters, etc. All of the men who had surrendered, with their eyes peeled and their ears to the ground, waited for new developments and news. Ghazar had assumed the role of a vengeful angel. People whispered that if he weren't captured, they would not harm us for fear of his retribution.

Hopeless prisoners! They thought their fate would be determined by Ghazar, while over 60 of them, young and elder men, were sitting like chicken in horse manure in the stables, waiting for a miracle to save them.

Who knows? If just a quarter of Armenians had resorted to defend themselves like Ghazar, the massacres would not have been so terrible.

I must mention here that, when Ghazar had surrendered his revolver and weapon, Takouhi from Mghsonts Khachig's family had given their own weapon to Ghazar. They were a poor family and people knew that they had nothing, so made no demands on them. Later, fearing the government, they did not wish to hide their small pistol. It was the only weapon that was not confiscated. Nobody knew, except for the people involved. Neither Armenians, nor Turks. So, thanks to Mghsonts Takouhi, Ghazar was armed with a pistol.

There was a risible incident one night, when they set an ambush and waited for Ghazar to appear. They saw something moving in the shadows under the trees, something that was heading in their direction. They aimed their guns and waited with bated breath. They saw a silhouette in the darkness and thought it was Ghazar. But, instead of waiting for the figure to approach, they opened fire. The silhouette fell, and they ran to it to celebrate their success. However, they saw that instead of Ghazar, they had shot a porter who had been stuck outside the village at night. They had killed their own porter instead of Ghazar…

Whenever there was a murder or a killing in the mountains and surrounding wilderness, it was attributed to Ghazar. Whether it was a policeman or a Kurd who had been killed, Ghazar was always presumed to be the culprit.

It was a night in late June. One terrible night, they tied the men together, in groups of five or in pairs, claiming they were taking them to the city [Palou]. Instead, they took them to the slaughterhouse, the banks of the Euphrates, where they tortured them to death.

The heat was suffocating that night. A little rain drizzled. We were in the open-aired "chardakh," [pergola] so we had to find cover. That night, we only heard five gunshots. None of us imaged that a terrible massacre was taking place. We were all awake. We never saw those men again…

I later saw the sunburnt corpses of my father and some others. They had been washed onto the shores of the Euphrates by the currents.

All five of the corpses were completely naked. They were at some distance from each other. Clearly, the monsters had robbed them. They had only left a pair of underwear on my father. The Turkish cowherds took me there so that I could see my father one last time. He was lying prone, facing down, with blood all over his body, one arm folded under his head, and a bullet hole the size of a Turkish *mejideh* in his back. The blood had flowed down his side like a red ribbon. When I saw him like this, with his corpse blackened by the sun and unrecognizable, I simply could not take it. I broke into tears and wept uncontrollably as I walked away. I was young, barely 10 years old. I did not think of dragging the corpse away, even if I could, and burying it in the sand or at least covering it with a handful of soil.

Oh, I couldn't… I didn't think of it. I couldn't have done it. I was too young, just a child. But today, my conscience troubles me.

This was yet another bloody page of my story. Another horrific chapter of my life. A lesson and an example for us all.

Ghazar was still on the run. He had operated the village mill for many years and the Turks did not know how to do it themselves. They therefore had to keep another man from his family alive to keep the mill running. One other Armenian man was also allowed to survive because he had paid a huge bribe to the begs. He was Ashukents Ago. These two were the only adult Armenian men left in our village.

***

All the men had been killed. All the beautiful women and girls had been abducted. Unclean and tainted hands violated the honor of Armenian maidens. The desecration of Armenians was the order of the day, and nothing was left out.

Armenian boys were taken into servitude in different places. Another boy and I were taken to Hashim Beg's "ghonakh" to look after his countless sheep and cattle. After all, the begs had stolen every animal that belonged to the Armenians in the village.

As for the elderly mothers and women, they waited in Toroyents house for a caravan of poor Armenian exiles passing by, so that they could join them on their way to Der Zor, towards oblivion. Towards the Sea of Geoljiuk, where the God of Death reigned supreme...s[*]

How many remaining women were in that house? Perhaps 20. But at night, there were 21 people there, because a ghost would join them. Where would this ghost come from? In the dark of the night, without any fear, it kept the women company. While most ghosts inspire terror in the bravest of souls, this ghost was friendly. It did not come in through the door, as there were people after him. So where did it come from? Perhaps it was living in the abandoned houses of the village. Four or five houses were his hideaway. They had passages that linked the barns together, thanks to which this ghost traveled freely – from Apoyents home all the way to the women's makeshift prison.

That night, it appeared again. It was speaking to the women, and they were all busy with their conversation, when two men came in through the door on tiptoes, without making any noise, and advanced on the group. When they approached, the silhouette retreated, but one of them ran forward and grabbed it by the collar. The silhouette turned around and tossed his attacker to the side. He hit the wall so hard that he immediately collapsed to the floor.

Then, pandemonium broke out. Armed men spilled into the house from the roof, from the outside, from the windows... "Come on!" they screamed, "Ghazar is in here! He's inside!" The beg's *paraban* [doorkeeper], in order to ingratiate himself with his master, came forward in the dark to make the arrest. But bang! A red fireball exploded in the dark, throwing the *paraban* back against the ground.

"Oh! I am dead! Help me!"

The injured man was carried out. He had been shot right in his chest.

Nobody dared step inside the house again. They encircled the building and waited for daylight. They also sent news to mobs in nearby Kurdish villages to More than 200 of them were advancing with shouts, screams and curses. The begs were enraged that not a single man among so many

---

[*] Lake Geoljiuk was a major killing zone, a few hours away, where tens of thousands were massacred.

had dared to approach Ghazar. They brought shovels and picks to make a hole in the roof and shoot him.

When the hole was made, the Kurds saw Ghazar darting from one corner of the stable to the other, and all hell broke loose. One Kurd noticed Ghazar's location and slowly aimed the barrel of his gun at him. But Ghazar saw this and pulled on the barrel, almost grabbing it out of the Kurd's hands. The Kurd pulled the trigger and the bullet hit Ghazar in the thigh. Ghazar was forced to let go of the hot barrel.

At this point, they saw that there was no other way and chose a direct method – they sent in Garabed, the Armenian man who had been working the mill and was a relative of Ghazar, to convince him to give himself up in exchange for a promise of safety.

Garabed walked in, holding a lamp, but Ghazar did not know who had entered. He was waiting behind the door, on the ground. As soon as he saw Garabed approaching, he pulled the trigger of his gun, and the bullet went right through Garabed's heart. When Ghazar saw that he had just shot his uncle, he screamed, "Oh, Garabed! I wish I'd gone blind!"

This time, they sent in Ghazar's mother, wife, and two children to persuade him to give up. They went into the house but never came out. Garabed told them, "Whatever befalls me, you will share my fate." He did not allow them to leave. If they had captured Ghazar alive, his agony would have been unimaginable. But they did not.

The only choice they now had was fire. It was midday and they still hadn't been able to arrest or kill him.

They set the house on fire, and within minutes, the flames and smoke were rising to the sky, as high as the top of the planetrees. The entire neighborhood was ablaze. The flames crackled and hissed like dragons in flight. It was midday but Ghazar was still not beaten. Had he suffocated to death? Or had he burned to ashes in Nebuchadnezzar's furnace?

No! The man who had fought back against a mob of 200 and had awed them with his courage had also escaped the hellish flames.

Ghazar was mocking his armed enemies who were now dancing around the burning building.

The beg screamed from above:

"*Oulan Ghazar! Dusharu chuk!*"

But Ghazar, down in the flames, ignored the demand, which only enraged the beg more.

In his underground world, God knows how, Ghazar had been able to make a deal with the devil. In the chaos that followed the fire, he had been able to get back to his passage and return to the last abandoned house, which was unaffected by the flames. He then jumped out, ran out of the courtyard, and slipped past the "chardakh" gate, which was ajar. The gate opened right onto the street. Everyone was busy with the fire, and the narrow street was unobserved. Ghazar gathered all his courage and ran out. He ran past the school and began his final flight. Nobody saw him except for one Kurdish woman named Ayishe. She had gone up to her roof to watch the fire. She saw Ghazar and screamed as loudly as she could:

"He's running away! Ghazar is running away! Get him, quickly!"

The enemy mob, forgetting the fire, began pursuing Ghazar. Within minutes, the village was completely empty. Everyone was looking for Ghazar.

While the enemy was combing the orchards, looking under every rock, Ghazar hid under a vine that was part of a thorny growth that marked the border between two orchards. This makeshift fence was as tall as a man. But a huge and tall Kurd from Alkhatian happened to walk by and saw a shoe-print on the ground. He looked into the tangle of branches, saw Ghazar, and jumped on him. The predator and the prey were engaged in a terrible duel. The huge Kurd had grabbed hold of Ghazar's hands, so the latter could not reach his revolver. The poor man was so exhausted, both physically and mentally, that he barely had the strength to fight back.

The Kurd, in his turn, could not reach for his own dagger, knowing that the moment he let go of Ghazar, the latter would reach for his revolver.

The Kurd tried to grab Ghazar's pistol, but Ghazar, with superhuman efforts, resisted. Finally, the Kurd decided to reach for his dagger. At that very moment, Ghazar pulled the trigger. The bullet struck the Kurd right in the chin, but Ghazar had been stabbed in the intestines. The knife was plunged into his torso up to the hilt. When the other Kurds, hearing the report of the gun, gathered around the bush, the Kurd was already dead, but Ghazar was still breathing. They tortured him terribly, then dismembered and killed him on the spot.

This was the death of a hero. His spirit went to join the countless souls who had laid down their lives for the liberation of the Armenian nation.

Part B

The Horrors Experienced during the Extermination of Armenians

"Yev Yeghev Souk"

Armenian blood kept flowing. The sickle cut down whatever it met. It was like a volcanic eruption. The mountains and valleys were covered in Armenian bodies. Corpses floated down the Aradzani [River], occasionally becoming snagged in the undergrowth on the banks, as if to be displayed, and then dragged away again towards the great unknown.

My father's corpse, too, was tossed into the Aradzani, and remained on the bank for several days. Eventually, the current dragged it away, and it floated off like flotsam.

***

It was August, the middle of a terribly hot summer. Fire rained down from the sky. The land of Armenia was deserted. The grain needed to be harvested, but there was nobody to harvest it. Where were the field hands? Where were the pickers, the farmers? There was nobody left. Nothing but grief and pain everywhere. Neither the bellowing of the cows nor the songs of the people could be heard.

It was midday. The chirping of the crickets was the only sound. The air shimmered as golden heat fell from the sky. On hot days like this, the putrid stench of the bodies was enough to drive one mad. One could not breathe. If one looked carefully, one could spy the corpse of a man, woman, or child in the bushes, melting under the searing sun.

God knows which Armenian's life had been extinguished forever at that very spot.

The song of Armenians had been silenced. For four months, the Armenian language had been forbidden. We, the children, had turned inwards, each of us serving a different beg or agha, wearing rags for clothes and in bare feet, making the rounds of the pastures with heavy and bleeding hearts.

We were cowherds. Our pain, like lead, was lodged in our hearts and had rendered us mute. The prospect of violent death dominated our thoughts. One by one we fell victim to beatings at the hands of Turkish adults and children. Our numbers kept dwindling. They would drag our friend a few yards away and beat them in front of our eyes. We would turn away and block our ears.

We were still alive. We knew that we walked and moved. To verify that we were still alive, we would sometimes pinch ourselves, because we felt like walking corpses. Our bodies moved as if they were automatons, without vitality. We could feel our pulse, but it was not the pulse of a living thing, but rather the pulse of fear and death. Who has felt the pulse of death? Not of natural death, but a painful and tortured one. I will not lie and claim that I can describe that feeling with my pen…

We had been sentences to death… Just little children left to their own devices. Our fate was in the hands of the Turks, and they did exactly as they wished.

My younger brother, Setrag, had been taken in by a kind Kurd. He was the only Kurd in our village who did not have Armenian blood on his hands, and who had not participated in any of the looting. His name was Bukoyents Msto. Despite his extreme poverty, he did not even steal a broomstick from Armenians.

When the violence began, my family wanted to save some of its property by hiding it in Msto's house, but he did not agree, because he had a kind heart and did not want to have an uneasy conscience if something terrible happened. He was always a friend of Armenians and always honest with them. He was the exception. At the time, I didn't even think he was Kurdish, because he had no relations with Kurds or Turks. In fact, Turks disliked him and called him *giavour* because he openly professed his friendship with the Toroyents family.

Armenians had *kirva* relationships with Kurds who had proved to be faithful friends over long years. When the Kurds had a child whom they wished to circumcise, they gladly handed him over to their Armenian friends who took the *kirva* oath.

This oath was similar to the act of being one's Godfather. And this is the kind of friendship that Bukoyents Msto had with the Toroyents family.

Even in poverty, he was honorable and dignified. We all knew he was poor, but he never seemed to be so in our eyes.

He was always taciturn. His gate, his behavior, and his demeanor all invited the praise of others.

Thanks to a happy twist of fate, my brother had been taken into servitude by this man in those dark and terrible days. Let's not call it servitude, because Msto did not want to exploit my brother. He knew that a conflagration was swallowing up Armenian children and youth. He rushed to adopt my brother to save him from the fire.

At least I had this one consolation, that my brother was safe. I knew that Setrag was very young and unable to work. With Msto, he would have no more than one or two cows or oxen to watch over.

I also knew that Msto would care for him like his own son. Even if all he had was a single loaf of bread, he would split it up equally among the children. If there were no external threats to his life, my brother would be safe.

This was no small consolation for my wounded heart, at a time when blood was still being spilled, the memory of my loved ones was still fresh in my mind, and the corpses still littered the mountainsides, woods, and roads. Instead of a large and vibrant family, all I had was one brother who had the same blood and who was the light of my existence. Oh, what a comfort it was. He was the only source of hope that one day, our family's star would shine again.

To see your loved one suffer, under the heat of the sun, in bare feet, running after the animals... To watch him hungry but not be able to feed him, to watch him naked and not be able to clothe him...

But it didn't matter. It was enough that he existed and breathed, that I could hear his voice and had hope for better days in the future. This was enough to inspire me and alleviate the pain I felt. The knowledge that a kindly Kurd was looking after him was a great comfort, despite the man's poverty.

We, the surviving Armenian children, retreated into ourselves and went mute from fear. Where were the field hands and field workers? Where were the happy songs of the cowherds and shepherds? Where were the peasants' sweet and heart felt songs?

Mariam chadur zarger Ourmio lerneru,
Megtin souroun g'ardzer, megtin karneru.
Ororou chourn antsank, yelank i Darman**
Our vor aghvor mu gar, anounun er Mariam.

Mariam tonir varer, daniku moukh er,
Achkere zahrour er, honkeru toukh.
Mi lar, Mariam, mi lar, achouit g'avrvi,
Kez bzdig garkoghin dnagn aviri.

Mariam set up a tent in the mountains of Ourmia,
One one side grazed the *sourouns*, on the other side the sheep,
We passed the Oror stream and went to Darman,
Where there was a beauty called Mariam.

Mariam had lit the *tonir,* there was smoke everywhere,
Her eyes were *zahrour[?]*, her eyebrows dark,
Don't cry Mariam, don't cry, don't spoil your eyes,
May the house of the person who married you off young be destroyed.

This song would echo in our minds, as if we could still hear it, and would even sound off our lips for a few moments. It was as if nothing was true and we were living in a dream. We sometimes wondered if the Armenian language really existed, and was this song really sung once upon a time in Armenian home , in the fields and on threshing floors?

We weren't even able to talk to ourselves in Armenian. We thought that our inner voice would betray us, and that we would be found out.

***

Two armed riders noticed us and turned their horses' heads towards us, letting go of their reins. They had blood-thirsty and brutal expressions. Who were they? Why had they ridden off the road upon noticing us? Why were they riding in the dry grass at such a hot time of the day?

---

*   Oror and Darman are the names of villages.

"Shush! Shush!" I kept saying, "Quiet, friend! Speak Turkish, or they'll know we're Armenian and kill us!"

They came closer and dismounted. They took our measure, then asked:

"Your names?"

"Ziulfi... Ibrahim..."

The riders, who were gendarmes returning from the caravan, left when they heard our Turkish names.

We watched them walk away with bated breath.

"Once again, we escaped with our lives, friend."

There were moments when we, the little cowherds, discussed our preferred ways to die. We had come to terms with our inevitable fate.

We would ask each other:

"Vartan, if they were to kill us and let us choose how we died, what would you choose? Sword? A firearm? Stones? Sticks? Axes? Drowning in the Aradzani? Being beaten to death? Garroted?"

And we would close our eyes and imagine the worst of all pains. In truth, every possible method of death filled our young hearts with unimaginable terror.

We all prayed that they would at least pity us and not torture us too horribly, that they would end our lives with one blow. This was the only comfort we could hope for, because they had sworn to the world that they would not leave a single Armenian living on this planet. All would be killed. And we knew that we, the few children, though still alive, would be killed after harvest season, in early autumn, when the work in the fields came to an end.

This is how we survived that year of 1915, a year that will never be forgotten.

"Mayig... Chem Gna... Shad en..."

The destruction continued. The criminals had devastated Armenian villages and cities, killing everyone – the old, the young, the children, and the women. The mass of notables had been arrested earlier, taken to unknown locations, and not returned.

There was no more smoke rising from Armenian chimneys. The endless caravans had filled up many deep valleys.

Faint footprints on an untrodden path were the only traces of the recent passage of an executioner and his victim, and a little further on, the evidence of the victim's final life and death convulsions.

In the thickets of *pahan* (forest), thousands of innocent Armenian infants and children, youth and elderly, mothers and sisters had breathed their last.

The Aradzani had donned a red mantle, and like a wild monster, seething and fuming, collected the corpses from its banks and swept them away to unknown destinations…

At every step, one came across the traces of recent bloodshed.

The beautiful brides and maidens had all been dragged brutally into the harems.

The doors of homes had been smashed. Even the walls bore gaping wounds. Inside, silence reigned. The storerooms and barns were empty. All I could hear was the mournful and monotonous chirping of the crickets. The ghosts of the dead were dancing in a circle around me… 1915…

The children and youth who had been forcibly Islamized lived with the terrible trauma they had experienced. Many became cowherds and could not swallow the bloodied bread they were given to eat.

Yesterday, a caravan passed by. From the refuge of my hideout, I watched gendarmes raping a girl. With my own eyes, I saw her mother being tortured. A small boy circling around her dead corpse, crying and screaming. Eventually, a gendarme grabbed the three year-old boy by his hair, raised him up in the air, and smashed him against a boulder so hard that the boy's skull exploded, and his brains spilled out.

With his last breath, he cried out, "Ma…!"

I almost cried out from horror, which would have betrayed me to the gendarme. But I bit down on my lip and suppressed my screams. Eventually, I fainted…

***

Sheep grazed in fields covered with wild, dwarf shrubs, thorns, blackberry bushes, rosebushes, and ferns. In those fields, the snakes and the large

Missak (right) and Setrag Khralian.

The bloody bridge of Palou, where hundreds of thousands [sic] of Armenians were slaughtered in 1915.

green lizards ran rampant, chasing each other and playing *jirid*. One could hear a terrible wailing sound from one of those fields. It resembled the voice of a child, someone on the verge of death.

"Uu...hh.... uu... hh... va... yu... u... yu."

"It's an antlered snake," said my friend, "it makes these sounds sometimes in the heat of the noon."

It was claimed by some witnesses that when antlered and rattle snakes lost the diamonds and "priceless gems" in their mouths, they screamed in this fashion, furious with the desire for revenge.

Tradition also had it that if one saw two "antlered" snakes that were paired up and interlaced, one should throw their hat at the snakes and make a wish. In return, the snakes would give a magical "priceless gem" as a talisman, and such people would become rich and perform all sorts of miraculous acts with that gem.

"It's a lizard."

"No, it's a turtle," said another.

"Heh... Ehh... Heh... Va...Y... Va... Y..." continued the voice, piercing our hearts.

"Mother! I can't get them off! There are too many of them! Mother! They're here, they're here!"

Slowly, on tiptoes, we approached the voice.

We had only taken a couple of steps when, in the bushes, we found an injured mother, covered in blood, lying on her back.

There was a black wound right underneath her breast. There were also wounds around her neck, and she had been disfigured. A large clump of her hair hung from her head, solid with blood that had been dried by the sun. Her blood had coagulated like tar.

Next to the dying mother was a three-year old infant, emaciated and naked, his neck so thin that it looked like a spindle attached to his torso. He had been reduced to a skeleton.

The child was leaning against the mother's half-dead body to support himself with a wooden stick in his bony hand. With that stick, he was removing the maggots from his mother's wound, which, like bees in a hive, seemed to be attacking her flesh.

The maggots had deepened and infected the wound. The child kept trying, making a supreme effort, to free her mother of them, but he couldn't.

Suddenly, he remembered his hunger and began wailing:

"Mommy! I'm hungry! I want bread!"

God knows when that child had last eaten.

The dying mother could hear her child:

"Mama! I'm hungry! I want bread!"

The mother could not move... She could not help her son...

Again, he grabbed the stick and tried to drive away the maggots, but in vain. So again he wailed:

"Mother! I can't! There are too many worms!"

The screams of this child and the pain of this mother rose to the sky like so much smoke, but finding the gates of heaven shuttered, fell back down to earth.

Mother and child were fighting a desperate battle for their lives. But death, without pity, loomed...

Terrified by what we had witnessed, we ran away – ran away from this scene of death, blocking our ears so that we would no longer hear those heart-rending cries:

"Mother! I'm hungry! I want bread!"

"I Weep... But I Succeed..."

In those days, to meet another Armenian was such a sweet experience... Only a few of us urchins were still living, scattered here and there as servants, and eating our morsel of bread with bitterness. We took great comfort in spending time with each other. Each of us would spend the night in his own agha's home, but when we awoke in the mornings and walked out of the courtyards, our first thought was to find our fellow Armenian boys. We would have to guess the direction in which they had taken their cattle and try to catch up with them. We would often agree to meet at a certain time, in a certain pasture, where we could all allow our cattle to graze. We sought each other out desperately. What a joy it was to be among ourselves! One has to experience it to understand.

If I couldn't find the other boys, I would not let my cattle graze. I would throw stones at them and scream, so that they did not get comfortable. Then I would find a high hill and try to spot my friends in the distance. I would drive the cattle towards any concentration of people and animals I had spotted, but my efforts would often end in disappointment. As often as not, the shepherds I had spotted would turn out to be Kurdish.

When we were alone, it felt like we were suffocating. It felt like there was no air to breathe, that we would die any moment. On the other hand, when together, we would share our strength and console each other. We still would not speak Armenian out of fear, but our hearts would communicate freely.

How unfortunate was the Armenian boy who had to care for wild and angry buffaloes! He could not come to the pastures and mingle with others who might also have wild and angry buffaloes. He would have to take his animals in a different direction, alone.

The Aradzani often split into forks that would then re-unite further along. Among these branches of the river was a large patch of grass and berries. We often used this island as our pasture. We would let the cattle graze there all day, and in the evening, the best of our swimmers would go and round up the animals. Each boy would separate and count his own cattle before returning to his village.

One day, after we had split up and were returning home, I noticed that I was missing a cow. What could I do? If I didn't find that red cow, Hashim Beg would kill me.

I handed the other animals to the boys, so that they could take them back, and I crossed the Aradzani by myself to find the cow. I was still young, and not a great swimmer. The boys told me to walk upstream for ten minutes, and I would find a ford. The villagers had made a cairn to mark the location. The current was still strong there, but it was shallow. If you erred and fell, you would be dragged away into the abyss.

I began fording the river. I was only halfway across when the water reached my shoulders. I thought of turning back, but that would have been difficult, too. Putting my trust on fate and the Aradzani, I finally made it across.

The sun set. Darkness descended. Dressed in nothing but a shirt and trousers, I ran around the island of berries, calling out the cow's name:

"Khrmuz! Khrmuz! Khrmuz!"

Fortunately, my shirt and trousers, which I had wrapped around my head while crossing the water, were enough to cover my nudity. But as I ran about in the thorny bushes, they were cut into shreds.

It was now completely dark, and I continued wandering about the island all alone like a ghost, screaming at the top of my lungs:

"Khrmuz! Khrmuz! Khrmuz!"

My voice would travel far and shatter against the mountains or blend in with the roar of the Aradzani. No Khrmuz, nor a single living thing near me. I kept walking and, eventually, my despair pushed me to breaking point. I collapsed to the ground, fell on my face, and began weeping uncontrollably.

I fell asleep where I had fallen. In my dreams, the entire island caught fire and burned. The berry bushes snapped and crackled in the flames. The whole horizon was lit up by the fire. Eventually, the river caught fire, too. I wanted to run away, but couldn't, it seemed like I kept retreating. The tongues of the flames kept leaping at me. I kept clawing at the ground, desperate for a way out of the conflagration. However, my feet seemed to be nailed to the ground. I screamed so much that I felt my throat ripping. The river had turned into a flood of fire and flowed in the opposite direction. Occasionally, fountains of sparks shot up towards the sky and licked the firmament. Eventually, an abyss appeared before me, and to save myself from the flames, I jumped into it. That's when I awoke with a start.

My heart was still racing from fear. I was half-asleep and half-awake, my mind still stuck in the nightmare. I told myself it had been just a dream. The night was cool, and the Aradzani flowed by. It sounded like a chorus of heavenly angels. I remembered that I had lost the cow and had come to look for it.

A thousand times I envied those who had died at once and were freed of new tortures. I, on the other hand, was crucified a thousand times a day, died a thousand times a day, and came back to life again and again, only to relive my suffering.

I tortured myself with these thoughts until dawn. The island was flooded with the August sunshine.

I stood to my feet, completely spent and weak with hunger. But I still had to find the cow, otherwise, my life would be forfeit.

I headed east, but upon taking my first step, I felt a needling in the bottom of my feet. It hurt. I saw that my foot had "made a house," meaning that it was infected. I knew how bad *khosta* infection could be. The boys who often walked barefoot suffered from it, and I had suffered from it previously, as well. The pain was so intense that it would not allow a single moment of sleep at night. There was no treatment other than waiting for it to grow and then become a boil. I would have to wait for the wound to run its course before cutting the boil and draining the pus from it.

I stood to my feet again and limped away. I wished the wound was on my heel, then at least I could've walked on tiptoes.

Still, I kept going, gingerly and carefully. I kept my eyes peeled, still hoping to find the cow on the island. Every time I spotted a reddish object in the distance, my heart raced, and I thought it was Khrmuz.

Had the cow drowned in the river? Had it been taken to one of the cluster of villages on the other side of the Aradzani by mistake (Giulishger, Armujan, Nor Kiugh, Nor Kegha Mezre, Nor Shunag)? The cowherds of these villages also brought their cattle to the island to graze, and the cow may have become mixed with theirs. I didn't even consider the possibility that it had been rustled, because all the people of Palou lived in abject terror of Teffiur and Hashim Begs. In fact, these monsters' names inspired terror as far as Kharpert and Dikranagerd, and even further afield. Who would have the courage to steal even a stick from Til?

So I deduced that if the cow had not drowned, it had to be in one of those villages across the river. Encouraged by this glimmer of hope, I regained some strength and began limping in that direction.

But how could I cross the river? I didn't know the currents, nor could I find the ford. I decided that I would take the risk and swim across. When I reached the edge, I tried to approximate the width of the river and tested the current. It was strong. I measured my weight against this terrible monster, which roared and seethed with huge waves, inspiring terror in any observer. I took off my tattered shirt and trousers, and wrapped them around my head. Then, in one leap, I jumped into the water. I fought against the waves with all my strength. Every time I paddled forward, the current pushed me 50 meters downstream. I swam with all my strength. In a way, the fast current helped me, as it kept pushing me forward. But the waves would occasionally overwhelm me, and a clump of my hair, not secured by my shirt and trousers, kept blocking my view. I couldn't see where I was going, and I couldn't free my eyes. Any hesitation under the waves, and I would be buried under them forever. There was also the chance of losing my clothing and being left completely in the nude.

I was like a reed left to the whims of the Aradzani. I battled with all my strength against this terrible giant.

I was closer to the other bank. Just 20 feet more. The current weakened. Another spurt of effort, and I was at the edge. But the bank was much higher than the level of the water because, in the spring, the river would swallow up chunks of earth from its own banks.

I was a toy floating on the surface of the water. I couldn't reach the bank, so I couldn't claw my way out. Exhausted and spent, I desperately grabbed on to the roots of a *madedag* plant. These roots were longer than two meters, hanging off the edge of the bank and reaching the water.

Grasping these sturdy roots, I breathed a sigh of relief. My heart raced, and every time I inhaled or exhaled, it felt like my lungs were expanding and then collapsing again.

I continued dragging myself along the bank, eventually reaching a point where the bank had collapsed into lumps of earth, with more *madedag* roots sticking out. I climbed over with all my strength, and finally dragged myself out of the river.

I was saved. But I was also utterly exhausted. I put on my underwear and shirt, then sat down to rest for a while. The nearby fields were full of melons and watermelons. Each also had a *khough* (small hut). The families who owned the fields would have someone staying in the huts during harvest season to keep watch over the crops. Usually, these guards were the elderly men, the women, or the 10- to 15-year-old children who were not capable of working in the fields or who enjoyed special privileges in their households.

I rose and headed towards one of these fields. I had no fear of the Kurds because these fields belonged to our beys, and the villagers were our begs' *maraba*s.

The pain in my foot intensified. My vision was going dark from

Manug Margosian (from the village of Nbshi in Palou). The first professional photographer from the generation of survivors in Marseille.

exhaustion and hunger. Still, I somehow kept on my feet and made my way to one of the huts, built in the shadow of a huge willow tree. Walking past the pile of discarded melon and watermelon rinds, I entered the hut, where a Kurd, sleeping on his back, was loudly snoring. With him were two girls and one boy, aged 9 to 15, sitting in a circle. In front of them was a huge wooden pail filled with *tanabour* [yoghurt soup] …

They were eating tanabour amid a swarm of flies. I addressed the oldest person, who was the son, in Kurdish:

"Where did you take your village cattle today? Hashim Beg's cow got lost on the island. I'm trying to find it. Maybe it got mixed up with your animals."

In lieu of an answer, he called his father:

"*Bavo! Bavo! Vorchu yov lajk ameyou manga e kho pers kennou!*" (Father, father! There's a boy here asking about his cow!)

The Kurds have a habit – when they awake from slumber, they rub their face with both their hands and murmur a quick prayer from the Koran.

The old Kurd lazily stood up and rubbed his face with his hands, mumbling a "Bismillah." When he looked at me and saw what state I was in, he realized I'd been through quite a bit. My face was swollen with exhaustion and tears, I was in despair from hunger and emotion, I was pale, and I was only half-clad. He asked me what had happened.

I gave him an account of what had befallen me since the previous evening, and how I had come to be there. Seeing that I was hungry, he ordered his son and daughters to give me a spoonful of their own meal. I took the dirty, wooden spoon, and I lapped up the tanabour from it, oblivious to the fact that both the food and the spoon were covered in flies and their eggs. When I finished telling my story, and the man realized that it was Hashim Beg's cow that was lost, he sent his son to the head shepherd of the village to ask if a strange cow had returned with their cattle on the previous evening. But the Kurdish boy returned without having found the shepherd and without any news.

Once again, my hopes were dashed. When the Kurd saw my desperation, he told me that I could go with Haso to find the village cattle in the fields and look for the cow. But how could I wander the fields in my condition? My foot was gangrenous, I was barefoot, and therefore, I simply couldn't walk in the hot sun. He offered me his clogs, but I couldn't even slip my swollen feet into them. Even if I had been offered shoes, they would have been useless. The Kurd made a quick decision:

"The donkey is tied at the edge of the field. Haso will bring it, you can ride it, and you can go together."

I mounted the animal, and with Haso by my side, we set out, not knowing where we would go to find the cow.

But soon, we heard the sound of flutes and drums. We had come upon some *posha*s celebrating a wedding. They invited us to join them, but we preferred to keep looking for the cow and asked about the village herd. One of them, the *ashuk* [*ashough*, minstrel], stared at me for a moment, rubbed his forehead, and seemed to be lost in thought, as if trying to remember something. Then he suddenly looked up, ran to me, and wrapped his arms around me:

"*Hey vakh*! Missak, is that you? Aren't you the son of Khralents Dakes? Don't you recognize me? I'm *Ashuk* Shako, don't you remember me? When we came to Til, your home was the first place we stayed. We put up our tents in the green field in front of your watermill. You were young, you would run around our tents all day…"

And without even pausing for breath, he peppered me with questions and expressions of praise addressed to my family. He didn't even give me time to try and remember him or to answer his questions.

"Oh, what a world! I never thought I would see you in such a state!" he said, "Oh, *Khoja Khral oghlou*, I never thought I would find your beloved son in such a sorry state!"

These moving words had an immediate effect on my already brittle state of mind. He was singing the elegy of my family. My spirit was already fragile and unsettled. My memories were still fresh, and so were my wounds. I could no longer control myself and broke into tears. All the pain that had been pooling up in my head now gushed out like a geyser erupting from beneath the earth.

I recognized him now. I allowed him to sing the praises of my martyred loved ones, so that I, too, could spend a short moment with the sweet and pleasant memories of my past.

Then, with great compassion, he led the two of us to their tents and said that I need not worry, as they knew where the cow was. On the previous day, when the shepherds of Nor Kiugh Mezre had returned to their village with their cattle, they had sent word to the *ashuks*:

"Go back to the island, a cow got mixed in with our herd. If someone there is looking for it, tell him where it is. You're close to the island and you'll be near the road. You'll then be able to see anybody that comes by."

Haso and I went into the tents. They stopped playing the music and gathered around us. All the *ashuks'* wives recognized me. Especially Shako's wife, who was tall, a bit skinny, but attractive, with golden hair and beautiful eyes. She was the most beautiful of the wives of the *ashuks* we knew.

She knew all the members of my household by name, both young and old. First, she wanted to know who had been killed and who had survived. First, she asked about my paternal-aunt, Shoushan.

"They killed her," I said.

"Your father?"

"They killed him, too."

"Sara, your stepmother?"

"She's still alive."

"Your uncle Vartan?"

"They killed him."

"His wife Sara?"

"She became Sulukents Siuleyman's wife."

"Your brother Setrag?"

"He's alive."

"Markar (my cousin)?"

"He's alive. All the others were killed," I concluded, as I could no longer proceed through this macabre list.

When Haso ascertained that the cow had been found, he considered his duty to have been fulfilled. He went back home with the donkey.

I knew that the *ashuks* had great reverence for my family and me, even if my appearance inspired only revulsion. I asked for one of them to accompany me to fetch the cow.

But Shako's wife would not let me go. She saw that my foot was swollen and instructed me to rest. She wrapped a roasted onion around my foot to make sure the boil popped as soon as possible. They sent the bridegroom, Shoukri, to fetch the cow. He was Shako's brother and was instructed to make haste, find the herd, and tell the shepherds that Hashim Beg's servant had come looking for the cow.

Upon Shoukri's departure, the women made a poultice and wrapped it around my food. Shako's beautiful wife baked bread for me.

Less than an hour later, we saw Shoukri returning, driving the cow before him. I had no trouble crossing the Aradzani a second time. Even the smallest child can easily cross a river hanging on to the tail of a cow…

My First Heartbeat…

A 14- or 15-year old girl sat curled up at the threshold of a door, her chin propped by her hands. Her beautiful, dark eyes were glued to the ground, but would occasionally stare at some object inside the room or wander towards the horizon. She was rocking herself with childish innocence. A terrible pain seemed to always be standing before her, chasing away the innocent smile from her face. But the young girl fought against the darkness that was determined to take over her heart.

Sometime later, the young girl, defeated, relented to her fate. Sinking into despair and angst, she began weeping…

The Kurds and Turks had selected the beautiful Armenian girls and had forcibly made them their wives. The most beautiful girl in our village, Satenig, was still with the other Armenian women, who had been gathered in a house and were waiting for a caravan to pass so that they, too, could join the gruesome flood to the slaughterhouse.

The beautiful Satenig, barely 14 years old, had not been abducted yet because the Kurds and Turks were fighting over her. Each side wanted to possess her. The Kurds would take turns visiting, pressuring her to pick one of them. Satenig would eventually have to choose …

This was the source of the pain that tormented her as she sat forlorn at the threshold.

How could she pick one over the others? Was there one who didn't have Armenian blood dripping from his fangs? Was there one who hadn't drunk

Armenian blood by the mouthful?

The unfortunate Armenian girl needed to be rescued from the clutches of the monsters. One had to find a way, since nobody had tried to abduct her by force, because that would have led to enmity and strife among them, and none would have forgiven the person who abducted her.

The Armenian boys were scattered across the area as servants and living under "Muslim" names. But nobody knew how long this arrangement would last. This was only an illusory security. We would see Armenian boys or children, one after the other, being taken into Muslim homes and given new names. They would be called Hasan or Ali. The families would dote over these children, constantly asking them where their parents had hidden their valuables. And, when they finally realized that there was nothing to be found, they would simply kill the poor children.

Satenig's mother fretted. Her heart bled. She would have preferred for her daughter to join a caravan with her and to share a common fate, rather than leave her behind in the clutches of the barbarians where she would survive as the living dead.

Satenig and the other Armenian women got together and came up with a plan. Since the Armenian boys had converted to Islam and embraced the "holy religion," Satenig could simply marry one of them and be saved.

This was Satenig's only chance – to marry an Armenian boy. Who knew? Perhaps she would be lucky enough that he would be the same knight-in-shining-armor whom she had dreamt of in her youth, the man who could rescue her from her hell and give her all she ever wanted…

Satenig's mother and the other women got to work. They had to hurry, while there was still time…

Naturally, any boy chosen as a candidate would have to ask permission from his agha for the *nikah* [marriage]. After all, by law, he was a Muslim and a follower of the *hakh din* [true religion]…

The poor girl, bending under the weight of her pain, imagined horrible scenes of being raped at the tender age of 14… She would be defiled, her honor would be trampled upon… She would become a dirty rag tossed into the street…

She did not yet know that her mother and the Armenian women had found a way to avert her horrible prospects in one stroke by giving her hand to the Armenian knight-in-shining-armor of her fantasies…

"Satenig, my girl, in order to save you from those monsters, we're going to give you to one of the Armenian boys. Which one do you love? Which one do you want?"

Who knows what went through Satenig's mind at that moment?

How had she uttered the name of the one she loved and wanted? How had her heartstrings not snapped, how had her tongue not fallen silent as she said, "I love M…"?

***

"Boys, the grapes of the Baboyents vineyards are the first to ripen, because they get so much sun. As for the grapes in the valleys, they are still sour. Today, let's take the cattle in that direction, we'll be able to eat some grapes. Our vineyards may belong to the Kurds now, but who says we can't have our fill of the harvest? Whatever happens, happens. Who knows how many of us will still be alive tomorrow?"

We were in the habit of counting the days. We had now survived for four entire months, a significant stretch of time. We considered ourselves lucky to witness each new sunrise and sunset. Never mind that one day we would pay for our lives with interest.

"Fine, let's go to the vineyards. The grapes are hanging on the outside of the fence like goat's teats. If we are afraid to enter the vineyards, we can just grab them through the fencing and get a few bunches."

We took the cattle down to the valley. The harvest had already been completed there, and there was no need to keep a close eye on the animals. They could freely graze up and down the gorge. We began loitering near the vineyards, like cats circling a milk jug. The bravest of us went closer and were able to grab one or two bunches before walking away and stuffing their mouth with their loot.

These vineyards had once belonged to our families. There was also a man watching over them. If he had seen us, it would've been the end of us. Some of the boys stuffed themselves with grapes, while others did not have a single one. While we were busy with this operation, the cattle simply wandered off and disappeared. I called the boys that it was enough and we should hurry to gather our animals. So, I began running down the plain into the valley. While I was running, I tripped over something and slid way down, suddenly finding myself on the corpse of a naked woman. I jumped to my feet in horror and ran away without another glance at the corpse. But my knees were buckling and my heart was racing. I had seen quite a few corpses over the previous four months, but I had not been so terrified by them. Encountering one unexpectedly had given me a proper fright. I ran away, but then I had a strong desire to return to the corpse and see if I could recognize her. I gathered all my strength and calmly approached her. I circled her but could not see her face because she was facing down and her arms shielded her face.

I bent down to have a good look, so much so, that my face touched the ground and my head grazed her head. I could only see her Roman nose, a corner of her mouth and her eyelashes... I suddenly had a feeling that this was the face of a woman who had rocked me as a child, who had wiped away my tears, raised me in her lap. I sat next to her and thought it over... Was it really her? I reluctantly touched her naked body but immediately drew my hand back. She was cold as ice.

I wanted to be sure, so I tried to flip the corpse over and see her face.

I was terrified of touching her with my bare hands and wanted to use my cowherd's stick. The corpse was so rigid that I couldn't use a stick to flip her over because her arms were horizontally across her face. She was solid as steel and iron in that position. Her elbows were horizontal and would not fold inwards. As much as I tried to tip her over with my stick, her body slid down the plain. She had already slid about 10 feet away from her original position.

Her blood had flowed for some distance and had coagulated. My fears slowly dissipated. I threw aside my stick, put one knee against the corpse's back, grabbed her by an elbow, and with one heave, flipped her over onto her back.

A terrible scream escaped my lips...

I had not been wrong. It was Oghida, the wife of my cousin Asadour on my paternal-uncle's side. Her husband had fought for the Ottoman homeland in the Balkan War and had died in Adrianople with his rifle still in his hands, fulfilling his duty to his country. And now, his widow had been slain at Baboyent's vineyard [*ekou*] in a barbaric manner.

Three months earlier, a Kurd from Mayman had abducted her and forced her to marry him. That village was two hours away. How had the corpse come to be in our village? Why had she been killed? Who had killed her? Her Kurdish husband, or others? What was the motive?

Who would know and who would punish this terrible crime? Had she tried to run away from the Kurd? Had he caught up with her here and murdered her on the spot?

And what a murder…

They had stuffed a handkerchief into her mouth to silence her screams. They had slit her throat with a sword, splitting her windpipe in two. There was also a deep cut from her breasts down to her navel. A clump of her hair, solid with coagulated blood, was wrapped around her neck like a ribbon. Her eyes were half-open.

But why had they stripped her of all clothing? Why hadn't they even left a shirt on her to cover her nudity?

The other boys had, by now, gathered around the corpse. They all stared silently. Our hearts were heavy. They had turned to stone and had swollen to the point of bursting. But we could not weep.

The place had the stench of death. We quickly gathered the cattle and left.

I was baffled and in shock. I kept seeing the corpse before me. My head started hurting terribly, as if someone were striking my skull repeatedly with a hammer. In the evening, I rushed to drive the cattle back to the barn, and in that disturbed state of mind, I went to the "ghonakh" to report and to eat a loaf of bread. I then visited the Armenian women to hear what had happened while we were away, who was killed or which woman or girl was carried off by the Kurds.

Usually, the women sat around, miserable and forlorn, their knees squeezed together, weeping over what was happening, and thinking about what was to follow. I, too, would sit with them, downcast, giving my imagination free rein as I followed the conversation.

Satenig was there, her head buried in her mother's chest, her eyes red and swollen from crying. Who knows what she was thinking in those terrible moments? Was she preparing a shroud to suit her misfortune and black fate, or was she weaving a bright necklace thinking about a rosier picture?

Nshanents Zano, a woman of about forty, whispered in my ear:

"Today, the dogs came again for Satenig and we told them that she was too young, that it would be a sin for her to wed at such an age. We told them that she would be 15 in a month, and you can come at that point and ask for her hand. One of you can then take her away. So, we've gained another month to save her from the *'zor-giuj'* dogs."

Then, coming closer so that her lips were almost grazing my ear, she whispered in a barely audible voice:

"My boy, why don't you marry Satenig? That way, she won't be fed to the dogs… [Don't let her *masum* [innocense] be fed to the dogs]. Isn't it a shame to allow such a girl fall into the hands of evil men?"

I stared at her in absolute shock.

"*Des ishdour ul aghgeg e…*"* [Look, how beautiful she is!]

I thought the woman had gone mad.

"Both of you are young. You're the same age. You're suitable for each other."

Was this Nshanents Zano speaking, or some kind of spirit?

"Talk to the beg. Tell him, 'I've converted to Islam. I've embraced the *hakh din* [true religion]. I will marry Satenig and she will become Muslim, too. Let the mullah perform the *nikah* [marriage ceremony].'"

And the corpse…?

"Sister Zano, what kind of crazy-talk is this? Our lives aren't our own. How can I do such a thing? Are you delirious? We're not even old enough. Today, we found the body of my cousin Asadour's wife, Oghida, near Baboyents vineyards, brutally killed. I can still see it all before me."

How could I play my part in a comedy while I was overwhelmed by tragedy?

"*Oghoul!* [Son!] Is this the first time you see a corpse? We're all going to be killed horribly sooner or later… But you are Muslim now and they may not do anything to you. And if they were to kill us all, leaving no Armenian alive, what is the harm of saving the honor of an Armenian girl from the brutes? Why let Kurds defile her virginity? Marry Satenig. Be brave. Whatever is to happen, let it happen. It will happen anyway. At least we

---

* In Palou-Armenian dialect.

can deprive the dogs of one pleasure. Don't let them deflower her. Let a baptized Armenian enjoy her… Beyond that, let the Lord's will be done…"

I hung my head and thought it over.

Before my mind's eye danced a hacked corpse and a girl as beautiful as light. One dominated my vision, the other my heart. One was terrifying, the other splendid.

I didn't know what to do… I could neither stop the corpses from piling up nor wipe away the tears of Armenian maidens. My only choice was to lie alongside the corpses and cry with the maidens so that I would not be judged too harshly by either. That would be my reward.

As I contemplated my options, sister Zano continued:

"You know, my son, when we asked Satenig which of the Armenian boys she loved and wanted, she chose you! It seems like she's had her eye on you since she was a child. When the girls were young and played together, each chose a boy she liked, and Satenig chose you…"

A strange warmth spread across my body as she said these words. It was as if my heartstrings had been broken. I started listening to a new voice that was calling me. As a sense of satisfaction overtook me, my heart began racing. I didn't even know what I was feeling.

I wanted to hear those magical, bewitching words again. The words she had uttered. "She loves you."

Of course, the Zano sisters' decision was final, and the plan was set.

I was still a cowherd. I ran around the fields all day, barefoot and semi-clad, like a madman, with an unfeeling heart and an unthinking brain. There was a grave in my heart covered by Satenig's veil of love.

In the days that followed, I would find myself lying beside many, many more corpses. I would pray over many, many more corpses. Instead of gaining a bride, I gained another source of pain. My recompense was always more corpses and more death…

***

Every morning, before leaving for the fields, and every evening, upon my return to the village, my steps would automatically lead me to a ruined house with a low roof. I would loiter in the area for a few moments, and my pupils, despite me, would yearn to find those of another who had stolen my heart and taken it away with her. Like spotlights, they would scan every nook and cranny, but then, upon meeting a silhouette, they would immediately slink back behind my eyelids.

What were my eyes so scared of? The silhouette?

Yes, the silhouette.

And that silhouette, every day, at exactly the same time, would scan the horizon from a corner of the ruined house, seeking someone with the same anxiety and beating heart, as if she had made an appointment with him. She would watch the road impatiently. And so, the silhouette and the traveler would steal glances of each other from some distance, exchanging their pain with unsettled and pounding hearts, until one retreated inwards and the other walked away.

These two survived on the furtive glances that they exchanged. In one's eyes was the pain of despair, in the other's the rage of guilt. Both had eyes full of tears.

Hitherto, both had only been scared of corpses, and their thoughts had been focused on the massacres, looting, robbery and murders. One had lived in fear of having her purity defiled, the other in fear of having his skull crushed on rocks.

But Zano and the other women had now opened a new wound. Unknowingly, they had lit a fire of hell. They should at least have waited until the end of the bloodshed and terror, following the orders for the annihilation of an entire race.

While the Armenian women were planning the impossible to safeguard Satenig's honor by marrying her off to me (forgetting, of course, that we were all already wedded to death), others were making plans of their own. The following day, upon my return from the fields, I heard the terrible news. A short and extremely ugly Kurd with a scaly head had carried Satenig off to be his woman.

The begs had given this Kurd permission to take possession of the majestic Satenig who, a flower bud on her stalk, was afraid to flower, while her mother withdrew to a corner, wailed, and tore out her hair. All the women were dejected and downcast, sitting together in deep thought.

Satenig had been dragged to join the army of her fellow girls and women who languished inside the homes of Kurdish or Turkish wolves and vampires, breathing the black smoke of misery.

The inevitable had happened.

Satenig had become the wife of the repulsive and bloodthirsty Msdo. In his clutches, she withered away like a delicate rose.*

When I heard the shocking news, I felt like I had been stabbed in the heart. My arms felt weak, I went pale, and I froze in place like a statue.

"They took Satenig… They took Satenig…"

This was such a terrible blow for me that I broke down completely. It seemed like my heart had stopped beating. All I could hear was an inner voice repeating:

"They took Satenig… They took Satenig…"

She wasn't the first or the last. The bottomless gorges, the caves, the fields, and the valleys were all full of bodies. Untold numbers of Armenian women and girls had been dragged to the ungodly homes of heretical criminals.

The sun continued to make its daily round. Nature smiled again. The moon illuminated the naked and cold corpses with its milky rays. The birds flitted about, unaware and indifferent. The nightingale kept singing its song, perched on the rose bushes, with its beak deep in the red flowers, drunk on the nectar of love…

But something awful and terrifying was happening in this bucolic paradise. A caravan of people, covered in dust, naked and barefoot, their feet swollen and bloodied, their hearts pierced and bleeding. A pile of corpses with their intestines pouring out. A mass of the dying moaning pitifully, flailing their limbs as they waited for death, which would not come…

I would see Satenig every day. She was sad and dejected. The edges of her large and beautiful eyes were discolored, her red lips faded and worn out. In this state, she was even more beautiful. I gazed at her with yearning

---

* The name Msdo or Msto (Khralian uses both) is short for Moustafa. There are several men mentioned in this memoir by that name, including the kind Kurd who took in the author's brother, as well as the cruel man who had charge of the author in June 1915.

Armenian children emaciated from hunger in the deserts of the south, 1917.

A scene from the terrible *Medz Yeghern*.

and love, and she gazed back with humility and reverence.

That dilapidated and ruined house where she was kept, which was a thieves' lair, and which inspired so much terror in us, had now become a pilgrimage site, and my steps led me in that direction, just so I could feel that shiver run down my spine... Men will go to unbelievable lengths to experience that one frisson of emotion...

And then, one day, Satenig disappeared. I walked by her door again and again at the usual time, but I never saw her silhouette.

Terrible rumors began circulating. Supposedly, Msdo had discovered that his *giavour* wife had been unfaithful. He had taken her away and killed her, and then had buried her body near the fields on the road to Baghin and Srin. According to the rumors, Msdo had spied on her and had uncovered that she had an illicit relationship with his brother Badri. Unable to tolerate this insult to his honor and burning with jealousy, without saying a word to his brother, he had tortured and killed her.

And thus, the unfortunate girl was first defiled, and then killed by her defiler.

Badri, unable to resist Satenig's beauty, had forced himself on her, and both men had raped and dishonored her continuously. Rape eventually led to murder.

The grave of my beautiful and ill-fated bride-to-be was never found. Perhaps her remains were consumed by the birds and beasts of the wilderness, but her memory will forever live in my heart.

Forced to Record Death Sentences

There were 13 of them – Hashim Beg's servants. The *sakman*, the *seyis*, the quartermaster, all kinds of henchmen. A group of bloodthirsty ogres. In the open-air pergola (*chardakh*), gathered around the huge flat, copper tray (*sini*), they had their evening supper. I, meanwhile, like a sparrow caught among hawks, struggled with my worn wooden spoon, endeavoring to snatch a spoonful of soup for myself. Greedily, they stole mouthfuls from each other, as if they would never be satiated.

Nobody attempted to speak, because with each word, one would forfeit a spoonful. I would keep my spoon suspended in the air over the bowl, until I could find an opening to sneak through with much trepidation and get a grain or two. Otherwise, I would die of hunger.

Nearby, near the balcony, Hashim Beg was having supper, too, with some visiting begs and three gendarmes who had just returned from slaughtering Armenians. They were also having dinner, like princes. The guests and the gendarmes were telling a story in low voices and with great enjoyment, while our beg burst into laughter at every word with ugly spasms of his face. This was a habit of his. His thin and wiry face, reminiscent of Satan's, would become warped when he laughed and opened his mouth, brandishing two rows of large teeth, sharp like a dog's fangs and yellowed with cigar smoke.

I was looking in their direction. I kept watch over them from the corner of my eye, and I had my ear tuned to them, hoping to hear their conversation.

One of his aides' head sometimes blocked my view of the beg and his guests. Despite my best efforts, I could not glean anything from their conversation. They spoke in soft voices and the clinking of 14 spoons made it impossible to eavesdrop. But I was sure that they were talking about Armenians. Of course the gendarmes were telling awful, lurid stories, and Hashim Beg was enjoying them tremendously and roaring with laughter.

I kept watching them from the corner of my eyes. They went quiet for a moment and then, Hashim Beg, who was reclining against a cushion, sat up and leaned over to whisper to one of the gendarmes, pointing out the sparrow to the other hawks.

"Which one?" asked the gendarme.

I heard the question. The piece of bread that I was chewing turned into a huge lump of dough in my mouth. I couldn't swallow it. My jaw began hurting and I couldn't chew any more. It was as if my jawbones had been locked. My arms went limp. My body collapsed into my chair, and I could barely keep from falling to the ground.

The beg was pointing at me with his finger:

"That child!"

I lowered my gaze. I did not want to see that finger pointing at me.

Why was he pointing me out to the gendarmes? What were they going to do with me?

The Horrors Experienced during the Extermination of Armenians

Was my beg going to hand me over to them for their pleasure, so that they could torture and kill me? They could've crushed my skull with a single blow of a club. Weren't they the people who wiped out our village and were now killings survivors one by one?

Therefore, why would they point out the presence of an Armenian child in the "ghonakh" to them, the gendarmes? To hide my fear and emotions from the others around the table, I stood up with great difficulty. I felt my knees buckle and shivers ran through my body. I was like a man delirious with fever.

It was already dark. I escaped to the courtyard and passed through a hallway to a large room where I collapsed on a cushion in a dark corner.

My mind was numb. I could not find the threads of my thoughts and could not think.

A voice called me and someone nudged me with a foot:

"*Oulen Kadir, kakh! Kakh! Beg seni istiyor.*" [Hey Kadir, get up! Get up! The Beg wants you.]

Silently, I sat up. The man speaking to me in the dark was Farugh, a horse healer from Alkhatian. He was not as bad as the others and often pitied me. Sometimes he would even comfort me with his words when he saw me in the clutches of despair or terror.

He reprimanded me:

"You left the table. Where did you go? The beg has been looking for you for an hour!"

He went on to say that the *khunzur* pasha was praising me to his guests and the gendarmes. Farugh had heard their entire conversation, as he had been serving their food.

This revelation eased my mind to a certain extent and my fears subsided. Saying nothing of my concerns, I followed him back. I did not ask any questions. I didn't want him to know how terrified I'd been.

Thankfully, they had not lit the lamps, and the twilight of the summer evening hid my face and their cruel faces from my eyes.

When I reached them, Hashim Beg immediately turned to his guests:

"*Ishde bou chojoughu dediyim.*" [Here is the child I was talking about.]

I didn't know what he had told them.

Arif Beg, from Charsanjak, who was a friend of our beg's and one of the guests, questioned me without any preliminary introductions:

"Do you speak English or French?"

I was taken aback. Why were they asking me such a question?

"No," I replied.

Upon hearing my answer, Hashim Beg lost his temper and screamed into my face:

"*Oulan it oghlou it!* [Hey, dog son-of-a-bitch!] What do you mean you do not know?"

Then, embarrassed, he turned to the others:

"This son of a bitch is scared to say that he knows English and French, as if something terrible will happen to him if he admits it."

It became clear that during dinner, Hashim Beg, without giving the issue any serious thought or thinking of possible consequences, had praised me to high heaven to his guests. Now, upon my negative answer, in order not to be humiliated before his friends, he attributed my answer to fear.

Was this murderer, who had killed my own father, now proud of keeping the young child of his multilingual victim in his mansion? Never mind that the child did not actually know English and had never heard French because the murderers themselves had razed such schools to the ground and planted barley in their stead.

I felt that I had made a big mistake by confessing my ignorance. I rushed to clarify to Arif Beg that I only knew a little French and English because I had forgotten it due to a lack of practice, just as I was forgetting Armenian.

Hashim Beg's face lit up, a demonic smile appeared on his lips, and he breathed a deep sigh of relief.

"You see, effendis, this *it oghlou it* [dog son-of-a-bitch] knew the languages all along but lied to us."

After asking me a few more questions, Hashim Beg ordered me not to go to the fields the following day but stay and accompany the gendarmes and his own servants to prepare a list of Armenians still alive in the village. How many were there? How many had married Turks or Kurds? How many had converted to Islam and entered servitude? And how many unmarried elderly and middle aged women remained in the Toroyents house?

My God. This meant that I would be joining the gendarmes the next day and personally preparing the death sentence of each of my kith and kin. I would deliver the list to the gendarmes, so that at the end of the harvest season work, they would use the list I had prepared to identify people by their full names and take them to the slaughterhouse.

A demonic idea engendered by the Turkish mind. They were forcing the child to sign the father's death sentence.

But it was impossible to disobey the beg's orders. On the following day, Arif Beg, along with the other begs and a gendarme, would be going to the city of Palou, and two gendarmes would remain in the "ghonakh" to conduct my work.

To ensure that I had no fear for my safety, and to make it clear that I was an exception among Armenians, the beg proclaimed in their presence:

"You know, this child is now a Muslim and has disavowed his Armenian roots forever. His name is Kadir. Yahya Khoja will be teaching him the Koran and he will continue living in my 'ghonakh' freely and safely. Nobody will touch a hair on his head."

Then, to stroke my vanity, he added:

"In a few years, he'll marry one of my *beslamas* [servant girls] and he'll be my *sakman*."

Yes... I would be his *sakman*, and with a rifle hanging from my shoulder, would run after the same swift stallion that once belonged to the Nanavartig family. Its erstwhile owner had returned from America and bought it for 150 pounds. His body now lay on the banks of the Aradzani, feeding the carrion birds.

The stallion of the Nanavartigs Manoug was famed across the entire district of Palou. Before the Yeghern, the begs had tried everything they could to take it away from its owner, but had failed. There was even an offer of 300 pounds for it, but the late Manoug had remained steadfast. But then, with one swing of the club, the white charger had become the property of Hashim Beg.

Naturally, as a *sakman*, I would have to keep up with the beg on his right side, always ready to lay down my own life to protect him.

That night, I cried until morning and did not get a wink of sleep. I cursed all schooling, education, and erudition. Why should I know my enemy's language, and why was I chosen to record the names of my mother and brother in the book of the dead?

I wished that the night would never end, that it would stretch on forever. I wished the universe would remain in that darkness forever, and so would I. I wished that the sun would never rise in the sky again, if it only meant that I would be spared this new ordeal.

The disc of the sun had almost reached its zenith. There was nobody else left in the "ghonakh," not a sound to be heard. I rushed downstairs to see Farugh, to ask him whether the beg and his friends had already left for the city, or whether the gendarmes were in the "ghonakh" to head out and register the village's Armenians.

I ran down the stairs and pushed open the door of the stable. It was empty. The only thing inside was the beg's special horse, which he only rode once or twice a year on special occasions. This horse's saddle alone, bedecked with silver and gold ornaments, was worth 25 gold liras. The horse was belligerent and aggressive, as it never saw the sunlight. Its body was like a fish, with completely even muscle tone. The beg needed four-five people's help to mount it.

When I saw that the stable was empty, I rejoiced. I realized that they had all left already.

Farugh was sweeping the huge courtyard with a broom. I ran to him to confirm that the begs and gendarmes had left and ask him for more news.

The *seyis* said that the grand *khanum* (Hashim Beg's mother) had not wanted me to register the Armenians because I would be accompanying the *kiuchiuk khanums* [little khanums] and maids to shake the almonds off almond trees at the monastery. She had told her son that in another few days, the cowherds and shepherds wouldn't leave a single almond on those trees. They had to be collected that day.

For the previous 15 days, they had appointed one of my friends, Nshanents Armenag, to keep watch over the trees.

Since the *khanums* were "namahrem" and shielded from men, not even my friend Armenag, who was my size, and in fact, a year younger, was allowed to see them. As a result, I was the only male who had free entry into the harem and the women did not hide from me.

When the beg's Circassian mother, Giulsima, had ordered that I stay home to join them, the beg had been forced to abandon his plans, as neither the gendarmes or any one of them could read or write Turkish. They had therefore decided to leave together for the city.

And thus, thanks to this serendipitous intervention of fate, I had been spared from an awful task. I was so happy that I could have kissed Farugh on the forehead or fallen at the grand khanum's feet.

The altar of the millennia-old cathedral was in half-ruins. And although its apses were razed, the proud dome towered above.

I was happy. I thought that all the saints and martyrs were watching over me. The altar of the ancient cathedral inspired me with strength and determination.

Have you ever felt the loneliness of your spirit when you are in the clutches of death? Has your being ever been traumatized by successive images of gore and terror? Spend time in the ruins of a monastery where you can feel the breath of saints. That day, I felt that breath, as I shook the almonds off the branches…

An Invisible Hand at Work

It was autumn. The days were bleak and dreary. The dampness seeped into our spirits. A terrible fear dominated our hearts.

The work in the fields and barns was finished. The countdown concerning the future of those remaining alive had also ended and we awaited our final fate.

A few gendarmes had come to the beg's "ghonakh." They were discussing how they would take the women who had not been married off to join a caravan. Those Turks and Kurds who wished to keep the Armenian boys and women they had taken into servitude would be allowed to keep them.

So, those remaining alive had prepared to take the road to death.

Around that time, in those terrible days of despair, my stepmother gave birth to a son. On the following day, she was supposed to join the caravan. What could she do with that "piece of flesh" she had not managed or didn't want to get rid of while in the womb? The poor boy, who would have been my brother, had to be drowned in the light of day, so that he would be spared the unrelenting, universal poverty and suffering.

All the women were gathered on the road, ready to leave. My mother was late. The women kept asking each other:

"Is she not done yet? It's been two hours… What is she doing?"

These words were aimed at my mother. Early in the morning, the women had advised her to suffocate the child quickly under all the blankets and bedsheets she had. The women, moved on by Kurds and gendarmes, were preparing to leave on the road, leaving my mother to verify the death of the child and calmly join the caravan. When the gendarmes realized that she was a little late, they became angry and began cursing. One Kurd, a murderer who had just arrived in our village, went back to fetch my mother. When he went into the house, he saw that the newborn was dead under a pile of sheets, but there was no trace of my mother. He immediately went downstairs to look in the stable. He found her hiding behind the barn door. Beating her with the butt of his gun and dragging her by the arm, he forced her to join the other women. My mother was hoping that they would forget about her and leave, and that she would be saved.

I was curled up in the sheepfold, cowered and alone with my pain. I saw everything that happened.

When I saw that the Kurd from Kghi was torturing and dragging my mother along, I began crying loudly. What else could I do? Hashim Beg was not at home, so I couldn't go and fall at his feet and beg him to save my mother. I had no hope that he would grant clemency, anyway. But at that moment, Teffiur Beg's aide, Yousouf Agha, who had been serving Teffiur Beg for 45 years and was greatly respected because of his loyalty, was leaving the "ghonakh" for some reason on horseback. I opened the door of the stable and ran to him. I caught up with him, panting for breath:

"Yousouf Agha! Yousouf Agha!"

He pulled the reins.

"For the love of God… In the name of Mouhammad's true religion…" I pleaded, "Save my mother from the caravan!"

He looked me over, saw my tears, and replied sympathetically:

"I'll save her, my son, because I often ate Melik Yeranos' bread. I owe a debt of gratitude to your family."

He turned his horse and drove it right towards the Armenian women. The caravan was already moving away. He stopped the gendarmes and asked the women:

"Where's the family of Khralents Dakes?"

They pointed out my mother. He picked her out of the caravan, took her back to the "ghonakh," and went on with his business.

My stepmother is still alive in that terrible country. She lives in Khapert.

The caravan left. That night, near Sarukhamish (a village in Kharpert), unknown men attacked it, killed the gendarmes, then escaped to the mountains. As for the caravan, they were attacked by a mob of *bashu bozouk*s [irregular forces] and massacred. Not one person survived.

It was said that the gendarmes were killed by Armenian fugitives.

A Visitor in the Night

Although we were young, we had endured such terrible trials and tribulations that we were physically destroyed. Our clothes on our backs had been torn to shreds. Our feet were bare and had become bloodied from the hours we spent walking in the dry and thorny stubble of the fields and pastures. Often, when the poor boys found clothes on corpses, they would take them off and wear them themselves. My feet were swollen and scarred from the thorns. Whenever I found myself near water, I would plunge my feet into it to cool them off. I would often collect pieces of cloth, soak them in water and carry them with me, so that I could wrap my feet in the damp cloths and not feel the pain from burns. The autumn sun was particularly hot and would burn us. It was as if the sun had teeth and sunk them into our flesh, biting us like a dog.

For 15 days, I had been suffering from typhoid fever. I suffered terribly. I could barely keep up with the cattle. My fever would often rise so much that I couldn't even stand on my feet. I would lie down under the harsh sun, by the edge of a stream, drinking and drinking insatiably, but my thirst would never be sated. The burning sun would still not warm me. I felt extremely cold, as if it was snowing on me. My teeth chattered constantly. I shivered like the flutter of a bowstring. I was nauseous and kept vomiting bile. When my innards roiled, I thought an earthquake was shaking my insides. It seemed like my lungs and liver would come out.

Eventually, after vomiting some kind of yellowish and green liquid, I would lose all strength, close my eyes, and become delirious.

Under the circumstances, my only comfort was the fact that my friends would take care for my cattle until evening. At night, I would somehow drag myself home, then go straight to the burlap bed on the roof of the stable and suffer in solitude.

In those terrible days, my friends were my only solace. They included Antranig Marsoubian from Armuja, who was in the service of Teffiur Beg; my paternal-cousin Markar; Toroyents Arakel; Nshanents Armenag; and Tavoyents Asdour, who was also called Anajenk and was the son of the sexton bell-ringer of our village church. These boys were all in the service of different Kurds in the area. We spent most of our days together in the fields and helped each other. But in the evenings, we would all retreat to our aghas' homes and would not hear from each other until the following day.

My younger brother Setrag spent his time gardening with the seven- or eight-year old daughter of his agha, Msdo. They were *jouvelegs* (non-farmers) and had no animals to graze, just a cow or a donkey at the most, which they would send to pasture with the village herd.

The garden that the begs had given Msdo had belonged to Nazoyents Sahag. He had been the only man in our village who kept a garden and had been cultivating it for a dozen years. When poor Sahag was killed under the blows of an axe, the garden was handed over to Msdo, the poorest Kurd in the village, who accepted to look after the garden.

Antranig Marsoubian and I would never go too far with our cattle. We would tarry near this garden. I would lie down in the sun, still sick, and Antranig would sneak into the garden, steal cucumbers, and eat them. Who was supposed to stop him? My brother? The young girl?

My fever gradually worsened and I was bedridden. I was very ill. The following day, I couldn't get out of bed. The sun rose and the animals began bellowing in the stable. The stable was about 200 paces outside the village, on a hill, right across the "ghonakh," and within clear sight of the village.

I was rambling from thirst. My tongue was bone-dry. I couldn't even move it. Although there was a trickle of water that flowed by the stable, already boiling under the sun, I could not get up and drink from it. At that moment, it didn't matter whether the water was hot, dirty, or even bloody,

I simply needed to drink it. I gazed at the bright water and burned ever more, as if there were a fire inside me. Water! Water! Water!

Below me, the animals kept bellowing in the stable-yard and chasing each other to get to the front of the gate. The poor animals were hungry and the horned ones were trying smash the gates and break out.

I could feel their bellowing in my bones and feared that they would be heard from the "ghonakh" and the bloody, bootlicking servants would come to beat me up in my condition.

Soon, that executioner of Armenians, Siusli Hasan, came at me, grumbling and cursing. Without even asking for an explanation, he began kicking me in the head. I was so weak and exhausted that I could neither cry out nor defend myself. The monster, thinking that I was deriding and mocking him, became more enraged and started kicking me harder. I remained on my stomach, and every time he kicked my head, my mouth and nose struck the ground and bled.

Once he was satisfied, he rushed away, opened the gates of the stable with some bluster, and took the cattle away, I don't know where...

When I opened my eyes again, I realized it was midnight.

I had fainted. My entire body was in pain. It felt like I had been tenderized like meat. I wanted to turn over onto my side, but as soon as I tried, I cried out in pain. As I had fallen on my face in the morning, I had remained in the same position. My clothes were sticking to the bedsheets, as if they were stuck with starch. I felt them with my hands and realized that blood had flowed from my mouth and nose, coagulated like tar, and stuck to my covers, while my shirt had hardened against my body.

I wasn't thirsty anymore. Instead, I was famished.

The orchard, which was adjacent to the courtyard, had a row of pear trees. It was autumn. The small *kochemur* pears were ripe and the worm-eaten ones were falling to the ground. In great pain, I dragged myself to a pear tree and fumbled about until I found half a dozen pears and ate them.

But as my stomach was weak and empty, I began feeling cramps. I had eaten nothing for days and had been continually vomiting.

Whenever I took a breath, it was as if someone was pricking me in the sides with a needle. Crawling again, I dragged myself back to my bed. I was in excruciating pain.

A Visitor in the Night

An hour or two later, the pain subsided, and I closed my eyes. I was only half-asleep.

I heard a voice. It was footsteps, and they came closer. I opened my eyes and saw an armed man with bandoliers across his chest standing over me. The man had bent down carefully to examine my face.

Seeing me awake and my eyes opened, he stood up so that I would not be able to identify him.

Softly, he asked me in Turkish:

"Are you sick?"

"Yes," I replied.

"Are you Armenian?" this time, he asked in Armenian.

"Yes!"

"Your name?"

"Missak."

"Which family?"

"I'm the son of Khralents Dakes."

He thought for a moment with his head tilted and seemed surprised:

"Khralents…" and he sighed.

"Do you know if Hashim Beg is in the 'ghonakh?'" he asked.

"I don't know," I replied.

I carefully examined this mysterious and strange visitor, who was broad-shouldered and tall. He had a sword hanging from his hip. His voice was bold and peremptory. As he spoke, he suspiciously scanned around him on all sides.

"Is anyone from your village still alive?" he asked.

"Nobody," I answered, "except for a few boys and women who have married Kurds and Turks."

"There's a girl from Baghin who lives in Hashim Beg's 'ghonakh.' Do you know her?"

"Yes! I've seen her and I know her. Khimatents Zarman. She used to be in the Kurdish village of Alkhatian, but they recently brought her to Hashim Beg's 'ghonakh.' There's now talk that a Kurd in Harpoung called

Nejib Agha of Okhou will take her as his woman."

"Do you know when they're taking her?"

"I don't know the date, but she will be here until Friday. On Friday evening, Yahya Khoja and Nejib Agha will be leaving for Harpoung. They may take her with them then."

He fell silent and rubbed his brow.

"You said you're Khralents Dakes' son... My, my!"

I did not have the courage to ask him who he was or how he knew my father and my family.

"You've been sick for a few days. I know."

I was shocked. How could he know how long I had been sick? Did he lurk around this place at nights? Was he alone or did he have friends in the area? I wondered.

"Are you hungry?" he asked.

"Yes!"

The stranger produced some oven bread from his pockets, and a little *torakh* (strained yogurt or *cheoklek*). He gave the food to me and rushed away into the orchards, instructing me not to tell a word to anyone of his visit.

I felt like I had been healed. I felt a surge of strength and excitement through my body. An inexplicable joy filled my heart. I thought it had been a dream.

Had an armed Armenian warrior really visited me just a few moments earlier? Had it not been a fever dream or my imagination? I felt mad.

Who would believe that there was still an Armenian man alive, with a sword hanging from his hip, who wandered the mountains and valleys like a ghost in the night? We didn't even think there were other Armenians left on Earth.

The sun had not risen yet. A newfound hope for the future seemed to ease my pain. The bread and *torakh* had given me strength. I came down from the stable's roof and walked over to the stream that I had yearned for so desperately the night before.

I washed off the blood that had run from my nose and had caked on my face following the beating I had received from Siusli Hasan. The cold water and fresh air woke me up and brought me back to life, but I still felt terrible pain all over my body.

Around this time, Kurdish herdsmen and field workers began talking of three mysterious armed men they had run across several times. These men would flee and hide in the undergrowth when spotted. They were often seen near the road to Harpoung.

When I heard these conversations, I pretended not to be interested in order not to invite suspicion. But my heart would race and I knew that something unusual would happen soon.

On Saturday morning, I awoke at dawn. I heard a commotion from the "ghonakh." I looked down from the roof and saw that Hashim Beg was yelling and cursing. A large group had gathered around him, all armed. Some kind of trouble was brewing. People were running up and down the road and there was a terrible din. I could not understand anything.

I heard Hashim Beg barking out orders:

"Run quickly to Harpoung, Mayman, Bouban, Alkhatian, Grdo, Gomo, and Anato. Raise them up, tell them to arm themselves and search around their villages!"

Something out of the ordinary had definitely happened. Clearly, the armed men spotted by the Kurds had killed someone, otherwise the beg wouldn't be raising fighters in all those villages.

I slowly slid off the roof and into the courtyard. I opened the barn gate and quietly brought the cattle out. Then, with the animals, I snuck out of the side door. I did not want them to notice me. I feared both their retribution and their questions. I feared they might have witnessed or heard the conversation I'd had with the man in the night, and if they had, my life was forfeit.

Soon, with the arrival of the other shepherds from the village, the fields came to life. I was joined by an Armenian boy named Kevork, originally from the town of Hoshe in Charsanjak. He was in the service of Mehmed Beg in that region's Geok Tepe village. This beg was Teffiur Beg's in-law who, alongside some other Kurdish chieftains, had revolted against the Turks in Dersim in 1916-1917. Furthermore, the Russians had advanced into the Armenian provinces of Lesser Hayk, and the begs of Charsanjak and Khozat and government officials had fled in different directions. Mehmed Beg and his brothers (Eomer Beg, Ali Beg, and a third whose name I've forgotten) were fratricides, as they had killed their paternal-uncle. Their father had axed his brother to death and they had been accomplices. To escape retribution, they had escaped to our village and sought protection from their relatives Hashim and Teffiur Begs.

Each of these begs had brought with them three or four Armenian boys from Charsanjak as cowherds.

Naturally, I only knew the boys by their Turkish names: Ali, Hasan, Hussein, etc. I only knew the Armenian name of Mehmed Beg's shepherd, Kevork. His Turkish name was Rashid.

The two of us had been able to share our pain with each other. In me, he had found the pure and unblemished spirit of the Armenian people, which had remained untouched despite all the terror, threats, and suffering.

The two of us would speak Armenian in secret and often hatch plans for vengeance against our tormentors. We espoused dreams and ideals beyond our limited means. Kevork's presence was a great comfort for me, and vice-versa. We freely confessed this to each other. We always looked for each other. He was a good swimmer and nobody could compete with him in the water.

When he saw me in the distance, he spurred on his cattle so that he could get to me quicker.

Joyfully and without any preliminaries, with his usual vulgarities, he heralded:

"One of the three is dead... One day, they will all be dead."

"What happened, Rashid? I can't wait to hear. Tell me."

"Tell me my *miuzhde*s (good news) so I will tell."

He told me what had happened and what he had heard.

On Friday evening, Nejib Agha, Yahya Khoja, and Ali Chavoush, the son of the Egyptian Hasan Agha, had left Hashim Beg's "ghonakh" for Harpoung with an Armenian girl at around 3:00 o'clock in the afternoon. On their way, at a narrow spot of Daragyan Valley, they had been attacked by three armed men who had ambushed and shot dead all three in the blink of an eye. They had beheaded Nejib Agha and the khoja and tossed their heads to the side. Then, after mutilating the body of Ali Chavoush, they had freed the Armenian girl, Zarman, and had escaped.

The begs and the Kurds were frothing at the mouth with rage. They had sent word to all the Kurdish villages to raise fighters, with instructions to track down and punish the criminals. But no trace of them had been found yet.

Many thought that Armenian fugitives had been responsible for the ambush. Others thought that the sons of Aslan Beg, who had been axed to death in Charsanjak, had planned the ambush to exact vengeance against the begs of Palou who had abetted the murderers. However, they were unable to find the killers and save their *namous* (honour) by killing three people.

This was an unacceptable insult for the begs of Palou. Sure, the abducted girl who was being transported may have been a common Armenian, the daughter of a murdered race, but their *namous* had been trampled, and there could be no greater insult…

For us, it was beneficial that they focused on this second theory. We wanted them to pursue it so that they would leave the few surviving Armenians in peace for a while. But it was impossible to doubt that the true culprits were Armenian. Clearly, Armenians fugitives had audaciously struck down the three men and had rescued the Armenian girl.

Much later we learned that the avengers had made sure that Zarman was already far away in the direction of Dikranagerd [Diyarbekir]. They had taken her to a proud Kurdish village called Mi-Ar-Van,[*] high in the mountains. There was an Armenian there, working for the *miudir*, who had escaped the carnage of the genocide in Baghin village. He and his family, having been acquainted with the *miudir*, had fled to his village and been given protection. Finding out that Zarman was alive and in the hands of the begs of Til, they dressed up as gendarmes, armed themselves, and rescued the girl, taking her to Mi-Ar-Van.

For a long time, the begs contemplated the possibility of exacting their revenge for this crime on defenseless [Armenian] youngsters and women, but then came events that made them forget all about their losses, the Armenian girl, and their plans for more bloodshed.

---

[*] Possibly Mifargin or Farghin, near modern day Silvan, on the edge of the Diyarbakir lowlands.

The Russians were marching on. They had already captured the upper provinces and had reached Kughi and Jabaghchour. The begs were preparing to evacuate the area.

For them, it was a day of mourning. They were abandoning all their possessions and glory, taking just a few horses and a small portion of their wealth, and heading for the depths of Turkey, towards Konia, Engiuri [Ankara], Akshehir, or Urfa.

But political events took an unexpected turn. The Russian Revolution erupted and flipped everything upside down, leaving the begs where they were... Whatever they had packed, they unpacked, and the Turkish star shone once again thanks to the Russian revolution.

The Haven of Mercy

It was a bitterly cold winter. The mountains and valleys were covered in white. The blizzards roared outside – snow and ice everywhere. One's spit would freeze before hitting the ground. Tree branches snapped under the weight of the snow.

The partridges would gather on the roofs, finding shelter near the chimneys and drying their wet wings in the rising smoke. They couldn't fly in such conditions.

Outside the haven of mercy, in that frigid winter, a mass of thousands of pitiful human beings waited, half-naked and barefoot. In the unsheltered courtyard, people pushed and jostled to get to the front.

In the snow, barefoot boys and girls wandered about, screeching pitifully:

"Mother! Mother! We're freezing! We're dying of hunger! Help! Help! For the love of Christ! For the love of God!"

Women in different types of clothing, with children in their arms, would cry out:

"Mayrig! Hayrig! Take these children and either keep them or feed them to the dogs!"

An outsider would be forgiven for thinking that these people were a mix of different nationalities. Some looked out-of-place in their Arabic attire and marks of the *haji* on their foreheads and hands. Others were in Kurdish garb, and a few in gypsy rags. They all cried out in the same way:

"Mayrig! Mayrig! Help! We're dying!"

One would say:

"If I stay outside tonight, my child will freeze!"

Another:

"I ran secretly away from my Turkish husband. He's looking for me, and if he finds me here, he'll kill me before your eyes. Help!"

Some did not know Armenian and cried out in Arabic or Kurdish.

Meanwhile, nature was raging, and the snow kept falling on these poor wretches. The gale would blow and pile up the fresh snow on their bare backs and shoulders.

People's hearts had turned to stone. They did not hear the heartrending cries and pleas rising from exhausted and helpless hearts.

These people had escaped death and had returned from faraway deserts, from Der Zor. They had risked their lives and escaped the blood-soaked homes of Kurds and Turks. They had come here, to this haven of mercy, to ask for some crumbs of bread and some rags for warmth. They wanted to cover their nakedness and shame, but few were taken in or received help from these institutions. Many would wait outside for days or weeks just to register for entrance to the orphanage or at least receive some dry bread or a shirt for their backs.

This was their second calvary. To get here, many had trekked through the snow and blizzards for days, weeks, or months, nursing great hopes, to become free. Now, they were being ignored, mocked, and abused by American missionaries wearing leather gloves and equally by Armenian missionaries and haughty matrons.

"Make way! Make way! You wretches! You dolts! Why are you pushing? Why are you crowding around, you rejects of the Turks? Oh mother, they are such shameless people. They do not even make way for people to pass. Go die, all of you!"

The speaker was a supposedly Armenian matron, wearing a Turkish *mashraf*, spitting venom at the miserable mass of people. She was perfumed and well-groomed, well-dressed and well-shod, coming back with a bundle under her arm. She wanted to cut across the mass of people. Every time she touched the body of one of those wretched women or children, she flinched back in disgust and pushed the culprit away with such force that a wave radiated through the crowd as people fell on top of each other.

Fate had also thrown me into this persecuted and emaciated crowd. I, too, was being trampled and pushed, and was pushing and trampling others.

I looked around, without any idea of what was happening in this pitiable place. My heart bled. There was no air to breathe and I felt like I was going to suffocate. I wanted to cut through the throng and free myself. It was better to die in the cold and snow, than grovel before the Mister Riggses[*] and missionaries for a piece of bread and a warm cover. Being a beggar is the worst thing in the world, and the philanthropists who were supposed to save us from the clutches of hunger and cold were asking for our hearts and souls. We would have to sell ourselves for pieces of bread.

Suddenly, the crowd went quiet, and all eyes were directed towards the balcony.

"Shush! Shush! Silence!" The Hayrig and Mayrig were about to speak.

In order to stop the noise and complainers, Mr. Riggs and his wife had ascended to the balcony to satisfy the crowd, if not with bread and blankets, at least with the word of God and Christ.

Mister Riggs, who had worked in Euphrates College of Kharpert for many years, was now the director of the orphanage and spoke Armenian with a heavy nasal, American accent:

"My dear children. Our pantries are empty. We have nothing to give you. There's neither bread, nor clothing. Nor do we now have any room in the orphanage. All beds are taken. Tomorrow is Sunday. Come to the meeting hall at 10:00 o'clock. The Reverend Brother Asadour Yeghoyan

---

[*] The Armenian copy says "Mr. Iggs." This is clearly a reference to Henry H. Riggs and his wife, who were long associated with Euphrates College in Kharpert. Mrs. Riggs died in April 1917 and Mr. Riggs left the region in May that year, when the United States severed diplomatic relations with the Ottoman Empire and entered WWI. Mr. Riggs returned to this region in April 1919 to conduct humanitarian work after the end of the war. We can assume that this section of the book is describing the winter of 1916-17.

will preach to you of Jesus, and you will be comforted with the Holy Spirit. Always keep Christ in your heart. Repent so that He may forgive your sins and take pity on you…"

One barefoot woman, reduced to a mere skeleton, was holding an infant wrapped in rags in her arms. She cut through the crowd and screamed as loudly as she could with her wasted lungs:

"You unbelievers, cruel and pitiless! You tell us you have no clothes, no food, no room in your orphanage. But just a few minutes ago, a woman dressed in a Turkish *mashraf* [sic, *charshaf* or over-garment] dipped in *lavanta* [lavender], came into the building. You filled her *boghcha* [bundle] and sent her off. Local Protestants like her have been filling their homes with clothes for days, getting rich off the pittance to be given to the poor. As for us, we've trekked from the Arabian deserts to get here, and you're starving us to death. You speak of Christ, invite us to your meeting hall to repent, so that your Christ forgives our sins. What sin have we committed? Tell us!" She then fell silent.

Mister Riggs and his wife exchanged a glance and whispered. This time, it was Mr. Riggs's wife who spoke. After looking over the miserable crowd from under her spectacles, she began:

"My dear children, as Hayrig said, we have nothing left to give. It's all gone. Pray to Christ to provide for us, so we can provide for you."

This time, an elderly man interrupted:

"The God who will respond to our prayers and provide for you can provide for us directly. You mean may God provide for you so that the reverends and matrons get rich, while we die in the snow and cold, hungry, naked and wretched."

I cut through the crowd and ran as far as I could from that haven of mercy.

I had been in this strange city for seven nights and had nowhere to sleep. I would spend the nights in the ruined homes of deported Armenians, curled up under a blanket or a sheet, hardly sleeping.

In the mornings, I would head for the market square and would stand in the sunlight to warm my freezing body.

Near the market was a mosque called Oulou Kala Jamisi. The orphans and destitute would gather there. They knew that officials and wealthy men leaving the mosque would scatter coins as alms. When they did so, the poor orphans would fight over loose change.

"*Allahou Ekber! Allahou Ekber!*"

The crowd stirred. People began whispering.

"It's the *vali* [governor]. The vali is coming! Make way for the carriage!"

The throng gathered outside the gates of the mosque made way and a springed carriage sped into the mosque's courtyard. People assured each other:

"The vali is a very good man. On his way out, he'll be handing out money."

The gates were closed behind the governor. Armenian, Turkish and Assyrian boys gathered outside again, pushing and shoving to get a better position at the front, so that when the governor came out, they would be the first to receive a pittance. Those in the back would often leave empty-handed.

I was still sitting in the same position. My back was against the wall of the mosque, my arms were crossed, my hands tucked into my armpits, and I was lost in thought. Two Turks close by, one bearded and holding the reins of a packhorse, were carefully looking at me with mysterious glances. I didn't know how long they had been staring at me, as I had been worried and lost in my thoughts and had not noticed them.

The bearded man was younger. He was probably around 55-60 years old, while the other was much older. They summoned me with a gesture of the hand. When I walked over to them, they addressed me kind-heartedly:

"My boy, would you like to come work for us? We will treat you like our own son and not like a servant. We've been seeing you here for several days. You're always sitting quietly, brooding. We took pity on you. We can tell from your eyes that you're a serious and smart child. Clearly, you come from a great family, and you're a victim of circumstances."

I confess that I immediately felt a fondness towards these Turks. They had friendly and kind smiles.

Up to that day, I had only seen cruel faces, and my blood froze in my veins every time I saw a Turk. But this time, I felt no such terror. On the contrary, I yearned to be under someone's protection, especially as I had

Asadour Kh. Tavoyian. The only living descendant of a respectable family from Til. He now lives in France and is married to Zarouhi Petanian, from Sis.

been starving, homeless, and cold for seven or eight days. I yearned for a warm bed and the sensation of a full stomach. I no longer thought about the future, I just wanted to live like a human being for a day, and I didn't care what happened afterwards. I used to wonder whether it was all a dream. Had I ever eaten well, or slept in a bed?

I immediately agreed to go with them, but asked about our destination.

"Our home in the *baghchas* [gardens], about an hour outside the city," they replied.

I was taken aback and became suspicious. Again, images of the monstrous Turk flashed through my mind. I was afraid that they just wanted to take me away and kill me, and that's why they weren't telling me the name of their village.

In order not to arouse suspicions or reveal my fears, I repeated my question.

"Effendi, where is *baghcha*? Is it a village or a town?"

"My son, the *baghcha* is the *baghcha*. It's a *yayla* (summer house). It's neither town nor village. Haven't you heard of *yaylas*? City folk go there in the summers and stay until the fall. They dry fruits, pick grapes, and return to the city for winter. Our home is such a *yayla*."

Another dilemma. Why do they say "our home" and not "our homes"? After all, there were two of them.

I naively asked:

"Do you two have one house?"

"We are brothers, my son," they said, "the house is split between us, but it's still one house. You will stay with my brother Moustafa Effendi." It was the bearded man speaking. "He will not treat you any differently from his own Badri. You seem like a good boy. But why do you question us? We took pity on you because you seemed interesting and serious. We want you to be free of your difficulties. We don't need a servant. We can always take someone else, there are plenty of Armenian orphans. We want to be your guardians. Would you like to come with us? Don't be scared. Perhaps you still have the fear of the Turk in you. We can't blame you, my son. But we're not like those Turks. If you come with us, you'll see what we mean."

Finally, I agreed to accompany these two kind brothers. Our path would take us right by the Haven of Mercy, but before getting to that orphanage, they took me to their home in the city and offered me a meal with four or five dishes. I had my fill. I ate so much that my stomach started hurting, but I still wanted to eat more. This was the home of the bearded Kemal Effendi's father-in-law.

The two brothers had business to attend to in the city. They took their donkey and left me there. They returned late, with the donkey laden, and the three of us set out for the *yayla*. When we arrived, they immediately heated up some water, and the *khanum* bathed me with her own hands, as if I were her son. They stripped me of my rags and burned them. They gave me new clothes because my rags had been infested by lice, which had been eating away at my body.

I stayed with these Turks for three years. They truly kept their promise and treated me just like their own children. Kemal Effendi had lived in America for 10 years and had only been back for two. He was a civilized and serious Turk, who had worked as a government official for some time. All Turks treated him with great respect and reverence. We were the only family at the summer retreat. All winter, I saw no one but the members of the two brothers' families. All the other wealthy Turks who had summer houses spent the winter in Kharpert.

This summer retreat was a paradise. It was located at a beautiful spot, with fertile land, plenty of clean water, clean air, and vineyards all around.

***

For three years, from 1917 to 1920, I had no news from the world and saw no Armenian faces. Rarely, I went down to the city with my aghas and returned with them to the *yayla*.

I only heard that those Armenians who had escaped from the Kurds and Turks and had not been taken in by kind families or orphanages had starved to death.

That year, there was a terrible inflation in prices. A measure (*chap*) of wheat had become a rare find, and its price had risen to 15 Ottoman pounds.

I was about 16 hours from my birthplace of Til. I had no idea what had happened to my brother, my mother, nor any of the other Armenian survivors.

Three long years had passed. My consciousness was slowly developing, and I had a strong desire to go back to Til and see my brother, mother, cousin and the other surviving villagers.

Just as the deer yearns for water, I yearned for them all, especially my brother Setrag, who was young and in need of care.

My desire grew by the day, but how could I express it to my guardians? Would they let me to go if I told them I was going back to Palou, my native land?

I first broached the subject slowly and tentatively with Badri. I told him I missed my brother and mother, and wished to see them again once more. Badri was very attached to me and did not want me to leave. In the winters, we would sit around the *qursi* [charcoal heater] and take turns reading Turkish novels and folk tales. My agha's wife, Memina Khanum, especially liked to hear me read the story of a hero from Malatia, Seydi Battal Ghazi. She enjoyed my annunciation and reading tempo. I would also read the *Mevlud*, which was a religious text.

Often, Memina Khanum would say:

"You've come to replace my Aghasi… He, too, loved to read…"

Aghasi was my agha's second son who had gone mad after falling in love. He had attacked and injured his beloved's brother with a knife and had spent time in prison. Songs had been written about him.

The family's oldest son, Ahmed, was in America. Only Badri was about my age, around 15-16 years old. I spent three happy years living with this family.

In October 1920, I finally made a firm decision to leave. One night, as we all sat for dinner, I told Moustafa Effendi and Memina Khanum that I wished to go back home to see my mother and brother, as I missed them dearly.

They did not oppose my wish and replied:

"My son, if that's what you desire, then you may leave. We will not stop you."

The following day, the entire family came to see me off – Kemal Effendi and his family, my agha and khanum, and Badri. When I kissed Moustafa

Efendi's hand, I saw that this 60 year-old man was weeping like a child. I, too, broke into tears. I almost changed my mind and stayed.

I bade them farewell and set out with tears in my eyes. I had not wept for three years, but these were tears of love, not pain…

***

From the top of Mount Masdar, I gazed at my home village and was once again overwhelmed by sadness.

I still had three hours to walk. I was full of emotions. I didn't know what the next day would bring – joy or grief? Who would be dead, and who would be alive? I didn't have the courage to enter the village. I thought the same massacres, cruelties and destruction was continuing.

I walked past our field in Pshmucher. I went down to my knees and, with great longing, kissed the soil. I was not thirsty but distraught with heartache. I sat by the stream and washed my hands, feet and face. I calmed down a little, stopped crying and stood to my feet. Using a narrow path, I reached our old mill, which was now in a dilapidated state. The door was shut, but I could hear the millstone churning, surely milling someone's grain.

I didn't take the road to the village. Instead, I went into our garden from the back of the mill and stood in front of our old home without encountering anyone on my way.

Oh, our family home… It had been completely razed. It was a complete ruin. The stones of the walls had been strewn across the road and had partially blocked it. It almost looked as if the garden and the house were the same.

Where could I go? I could go to the Toroyents home, where three years earlier, the Armenian women were kept, including my mother who had been taken out of the deportation caravan by Yousouf Agha.

Were they still there?

Ahead of me, I saw a woman bent over, carrying two buckets of water, and I followed her steps. I recognized her from behind and my heart was pounding. She was my paternal-uncle Vartan's wife, Sara, who had become Sulukents Siuleyman's wife.

I paused for a moment. I didn't want her to see me. I was in the middle of the village, but nobody had seen me yet. Who was left in the village, anyway? After massacring the Armenians, there were 10-15 Kurdish families, and a few newcomers.

There was a boy playing outside the school and church. He ran away when he saw me. I did not recognize him.

But he had recognized me immediately and ran to my mother and other Armenians to give them the news. I thought he'd run because he thought I was an outsider and was afraid.

When I reached the house, my stepmother and several other women were coming out to greet me. My mother embraced and kissed me, and wept. I wept, too.

The news of my return immediately spread around the village. Armenian children and women came to welcome me, as did the Kurds. Setrag was in the fields and returned late. When he had been told about my return, he had not believed the news. They were all convinced that I had been killed or died. My mother said, "I went looking for you so many times in the orphanages of Kharpert but didn't find you. So many times, I sent people after you, and they came back and said that you had been killed. Some had supposedly seen your corpse, and we gave up any hope of seeing you."

Oh, the longing of two brothers for each other… We embraced with the tears of happiness and wept in each other's arms.

A Kurdish girl, who had been a childhood friend of mine, came with my mother to welcome me. She asked me about my three years away and wanted to know what I'd done. She laughed heartily when I responded.

She laughed because my accent, my dialect, and my speech had changed. I had adopted the Kharpert dialect of Turkish. I had completely forgotten the Palou dialect. She laughed because she was amused by my more refined and polished Turkish.

My stepmother and the rest all advised me to go see Hashim Beg and ask for his forgiveness for my sudden departure or escape.

Afterwards, I would have to find a way to make a living. My mother was no longer living in Teffiur Beg's "ghonakh." She had been set free. The other Armenian women eked out a living doing whatever they could.

My brother's agha, the kind Bukoyents Msdo, had died. Setrag had been taken in by another Kurd, even poorer. They barely had enough food to eat. My cousin Markar was still in the service of Teffiur Beg.

I was to visit Hashim Beg the next day, but the memories of 1915 were still vivid in my mind. I felt the same fear. I couldn't stand being near these bloodthirsty begs. I didn't want to see their faces and did not want to enter their obscene premises. But I had to.

When I entered the "divan," I found a lone Kurd there, whom I didn't recognize. He was the beg's guard. I asked if Hashim Beg was at home, and whether I could see him.

"Who is that?"

The *sakman* opened the door. As soon as I saw Hashim Beg's face, my heart began racing. But in order not to betray myself, I walked over to him audaciously to kiss his hand. I knew that if he refused my gesture, it meant that he was still angry with me.

But when I approached him, he opened his large mouth and burst into laughter. I bent down and kissed his hand, then took two steps back, and with my arms crossed on my chest, waited for him to speak.

"Welcome, Khralian. Where have you been? We heard that you were dead, but you're still among the living…"

He asked me a few questions and I replied politely. He, too, began to laugh like the Kurdish girl, and said:

"You've become a real *Kharpertsi* [native of Kharpert]."

I was lucky that I had touched his soft-spot and that he was talking to me in a friendly manner.

My fear completely vanished. Taking advantage of his good mood, I asked him to keep whatever wealth or lands he had taken from my family, and let me at least have the mill so that I could make a living.

Without any objections, he promised to return the mill to me, on the condition that I repaired it so that it would operate properly.

Having been left to the Kurds, and due to the lack of any others in the village with the knowledge to maintain it, the mill had fallen into disrepair, and many took their wheat to mill in other villages. That flour was nothing like the real thing. It looked like *tsavar* [bulgur], the grains cut into two or three large pieces. It was impossible to bake bread with it. The water tank

Garabed Bedigian, from Khoshmat village of Palou. He currently lives in Providence (United States).

was also damaged, and water shot out from all sides of it. The mechanism that moved the millstone was broken. The brass hinge that allowed the stone to turn and functioned as an axle had worn away. Everything was in a dilapidated state.

It was this ruined mill that the bey was giving back to me. As if it were his property to give to anyone…

They handed me the key and I went to survey the damage. When I saw that everything was destroyed, I lost heart. I didn't think I was capable of repairing it. How would I manage to fix all of the problems on my own? Then, I had an idea.

This was the perfect opportunity to rescue Markar from Teffiur Beg's clutches. They were also well-aware that a single man could not operate the mill. One person had to control the water flow while the other had to direct the mechanism from above.

I rushed to tell Hashim Beg that the mill had been seriously damaged, and that one person couldn't repair it alone. I asked him to assign my cousin to help me. The beg also needed the mill to operate, so he agreed.

In this way, I was able to free my cousin. Only my brother was left, and I knew that I would think of a way to free him as well.

First, I had to justify the hope that had been placed in me by the begs. I knew I would gain their respect if I did, and it would behoove me to ingratiate myself with them.

I worked hard and was able to repair the mill. Now I was the apple of everyone's eye. I became very popular and nobody would dare deny me a favor.

My mother no longer needed to work. The income from the mill was plenty, and we lived well.

My paternal-uncle's wife, who had become Sulukents Siuleyman's wife, had a daughter called Jouhar, who had been living with her. She was now of age, 14 years old. Siuleyman wanted her to marry his nephew Hussein, but I wanted to get her away to Kharpert and place her in an orphanage.

Since my standing was high, due to my work at the mill, I could do anything through the begs. First, I freed my brother from his Kurdish master. I could keep him and he did not need to work. He stayed with me for a few weeks and then I sent him to an orphanage in Kharpert. It was now Jouhar's turn. One day, I said to Siuleyman:

"Uncle, you know, according to the law, I am the master of my uncle's daughter Jouhar.* Since her mother is married to you, and her daughter is not of age, I am her guardian. I respect you as an uncle, and you must recognize me as your nephew. Therefore, you should not refuse me and should send Jouhar to my care."

He replied mockingly:

"Ha ha! *It oghlou it!* [Dog son-of-a-bitch] Who taught you those laws? Who put that tongue in your mouth to tell me the law? Three years in Kharpert and now you are a smart ass? Hmm? Is it because Armenians are free now that your tongues waggle and you talk loudly?"

Seven or eight months passed. I forgot about Jouhar. It was not smart to take a young girl under my care. I realized that it would have been wrong to separate her from her mother. But there was always the danger that they would force her to marry Hussein.

Jouhar was extremely beautiful. If I had taken her in, instead of one enemy, I would have made a thousand enemies, and my own life would have been in danger. It was better that she stayed where she was and marry Hussein.

But one day, Hashim Beg summoned me, and announced:

"You must take in your niece. That is my order. Now! No delays! Go take her home!"

I was completely shocked. I knew that this event did not augur well. Why was a beg involving himself in such an insignificant issue, a family issue, especially as we had not asked him to intervene? Clearly, he had an ulterior motive.

I tried to protest:

"Beg, I can't keep the girl. Moreover, she doesn't want to leave her mother and stepfather. Let her stay where she is."

"No! I'm telling you, I'm ordering you to take her in!" he screamed, enraged.

---

* The reference here is to Missak's paternal-uncle, Vartan Khralian, who was Jouhar's natural father. When Vartan was murdered in June 1915, Sulukents Siuleyman took Vartan's wife as his own.

I could no longer protest. I had to obey.

Against my wishes, he sent the *sakman* to the Sulukents house and had the girl brought to our home.

I returned to the mill immediately. I was distracted. I sensed that some kind of disgrace loomed over me. Soon, I became impatient and headed home.

I saw that Jouhar was sitting with my mother and the other Armenian women, looking miserable. I didn't want to see her or speak to her. The women had all guessed that something terrible would happen, that a storm was about to erupt.

"Mother," I said, "we can't all squeeze into this house. Take the *poti* (furniture) and let's go live elsewhere. Thank God, there are lots of empty houses."

My mother and I left, but I did not want to take Jouhar with us. I told her to stay there, that we would visit every morning, and only go home to sleep at night.

The three of us – my mother, Markar, and I – settled down in the house of our late teacher. My mother would spend the days at the Toroyents house. Markar and I would spend the days in the mill. The two of us also took turns sleeping in the mill.

Soon, we realized that an Armenian woman with a disreputable past, our own Godmother, was reporting everything we did to the beg. We all knew that whatever she and the beg were plotting had to do with Jouhar.

One day, this woman made an announcement to Apoyents Yeghsa:

"Tonight, Hashim Beg will come for Jouhar… Don't be scared. Be careful. He will not touch your daughters. His eye is on Jouhar. Be careful and open the door when he knocks. Otherwise, it will be bad, and you won't be spared his wrath."

The terrible news spread quickly. But for some reason, they kept it from me.

Markar was spending that night in the mill. I was in our new home with my mother. It was a night of fear and terror. Everyone waited for the hammer to fall, except for me, who slept soundly.

That night, when they went to bed, they reinforced their doors by piling chairs and furniture behind them and keeping vigil. They all shook with fear. Jouhar awaited her fate with trepidation. At midnight, the debauched beast knocked on the door.

It was not possible to escape Hashim Beg's wrath.

Just then, someone went to open the door, while the others helped Jouhar escape up the chimney. By the time the door was open, Jouhar was on the roof.

The beg stormed in, looking for her.

"Where's the Khralents girl?" he roared. "Tell me now, or I'll kill you all like animals."

"She's not here," they replied, "they've moved, they are elsewhere. The girl is with them or at the mill."

The beg did not believe them and searched every nook and cranny, including the barns and stables. Disappointed, he bore a grudge against me and ordered the women not to say a word about his visit to anyone.

Jouhar, meanwhile, jumped down from the roof and ran to the mill. Markar, seeing her terrible condition and hearing her awful story, took her in.

Jouhar's aunt was married to a Kurd in Najaran and they planned an escape to Najaran, which was two-and-a-half hours from our village.

Markar shut the door of the mill. At midnight, he whisked Jouhar away to his aunt in Najaran and was back by dawn. Nobody knew what he had done.

In the morning, when I went to the mill, I saw that something was bothering Markar. But I didn't think of asking why, and he said nothing to me.

I was told nothing of these developments until that evening, when we were about to go home to have dinner. On the way, he told me the tragedy of the previous evening and how he had smuggled Jouhar to his aunt's in Najaran.

"Why didn't you tell me anything all day?" I admonished him.

"We didn't want you to be mixed up in this because the begs and Kurds are all against you now and do not approve of your conduct. They think you convinced Toroyents Garabed to run away to Kharpert. Same with Nshanents Armenag and Tavoyents Asadour. They hold you responsible for all the runaways. They say that the Armenian children and women were loyal and docile until your return. Since your return, you have turned them

The Haven of Mercy

and sent them off to Kharpert, one by one. You took in your brother from the Kurd and sent him to the orphanage. You took me in. For these reasons, they have issues with you and I was afraid that they might hurt you. We did not want them to blame you for the Jouhar incident. That is why we didn't want you to hear about it. We were scared that you would do something rash and put your own life in danger."

Only then did I realize how I had been left in the dark and had no idea of what was going on.

I knew that Jouhar's escape would not go unnoticed. Hashim Beg would not simply accept it. An Armenian son-of-a-bitch taking a girl away from him. Would the beg, who was feared by thousands, forgive such an insult? Certainly not!

I also knew that they would blame me for Jouhar's escape, no matter that I only found out about it after the incident. The storm would erupt, sooner or later.

I stayed in the mill that night. Dawn had just broken in the morning, and I had just finished milling grain for some Kurds. I was filling a bag with flour when the beg's mule keeper burst in. He was a Kurd from Bouban. He grabbed me by the arm and pulled me aside.

"Quick! The beg wants to see you now!"

He didn't even let me finish measuring the grain I was pouring. He dragged me away by the arm, as if he thought I would run away if he let go. I realized that I was in serious trouble. As we entered the "ghonakh," my knees buckled. He threw open the gate of the barn, threw me inside, then locked me in.

I saw that Markar was already there. They had dragged him there from his bed at home. Both of us were in limbo, floating between life and death. We couldn't say anything to comfort each other. We had gone mute with fear. The beg's curses and screams rose to high heaven from the *divan*. I had no idea why he was so enraged.

There were many official guests at the "ghonakh" that day. They all left. We could hear the neighing of their horses from our prison cell.

Soon, we heard footsteps coming down the stairs. Markar quickly gathered whatever clubs, axes, sticks and shovels he could see, and hid them in a corner. We didn't want our captors to beat us with them. We knew that the beg favored beating his victims to death. He had beaten a Kurd to death in 1914 and I had not forgotten it. Now it was our turn, two orphaned brothers.

The footsteps came to a halt right outside the barn. He unlocked the door with some bluster and we were confronted by the silhouette of our executioner.

He had a stick in his hand, specially cut and polished. It looked like it had been extracted from a snake's mouth. It had a tasseled strap that went through a hole in the handle and was wrapped around his wrist. In his other hand, he held a plate, and with a finger he was stirring its contents. His yellow eyes sought us out in the dark. When he spotted me, he spoke:

"Khral oghli, bouraya gel..." [Son of Khral, come here].

I stood up with some difficulty. My knees buckled but I somehow approached him. He stuck the plate practically into my eyes.

"What is this?"

It was a plate of bran left after milling flour.

He repeated:

"What is this?"

"Beg, it's flour bran," I replied, but my lips trembled, and my heart was beating so hard that I thought my ribs would break.

"Is this barley or wheat bran? You have mixed barley with the wheat, no?"

"No, beg. Why would I mix barley with wheat? How is that possible? They recently hardened the millstone. Perhaps the flour was ground too coarse and that's why it got mixed with some bran."

"Are you saying I'm lying, *khunzir kyafir giavour oghlu giavour?*" [pig unbeliever, son of an unbeliever].

He then tossed the plate as far as he could, he grabbed hold of my arm violently, and began beating me mercilessly with his stick.

I screamed, I cried, I tried to shake him off. Every time I slipped away, he struck my bare ankles to make sure I couldn't escape. He hit my body and feet until I lay on the ground, unconscious. The last thing I heard was Markar's cry, "Oh, mother!" and then I blacked out.

When I opened my eyes, it was very late, and I was on the bed at the mill. My clothes and body were wet. I didn't know who had brought me there. Five minutes later, one of the beg's servants approached me and saw that I was awake.

"Get up!" he said, "You have to leave. You have to leave the village immediately."

I asked the servant who had brought me to the mill and why my clothes were wet.

"You passed out," he replied. "We had to douse you with water. Afterwards, you walked here."

It was strange. I had no memory of walking to the mill. It was just like a dream that I had forgotten. I also had no memory of the beating I had just endured.

"Quickly, get off the bed. Your mother and cousin are waiting for you downstairs. You have to leave right away!" he said, peremptorily.

The sun had set. I walked out of the mill. My mother and Markar were waiting for me on the road. The mule keeper from Bouban was there, too. We three unfortunates were joined by two Kurds who escorted us out of the village.

After beating us savagely, Hashim Beg had sent someone to kick my mother out of our house, seal the door with wax, and bring her to join us.

The Kurds advised us to never return to the village. The beg had announced that he would raze the house of anyone who gave us shelter.

The Kurds returned to the village and we were left in a valley. Where could we go? What were we to do? I was in a terrible state. My entire body was in pain. My bones had been shattered. My mother said:

"It's still hot, you're not feeling the real pain yet. The real pain will come later."

We had to find shelter before nightfall.

We decided that I should go to Turkhe. A distant relation of ours, a girl named Osgeg, had married a Kurd from that village. It was barely half an hour away from our village. They would sneak back into our village at nightfall and shelter with one of our Kurdish neighbors. I advised them to abandon this plan, fearful that they would be betrayed, but what else could they do? My mother said that she would go to Osoyents Ayishe's house and nobody would see her there. Markar would also go there until daylight.

My body felt heavier and number by the minute. There was no time to lose. Already, the pain in my ribs made it difficult to breathe. I set out for Turkhe and went to the Kurd's house.

It was completely dark. The Kurdish husband was not at home. Oskeg was busy putting her two children to sleep. She had two sons with the Kurd. When she saw me, she greeted me in Kurdish:

"Kheru zie, kanjara yenni, unne shovura?" (Welcome! Where are you coming from like this, at night?]

I told her my misfortune. She was moved to tears. She immediately got some flour, kneaded dough, made some poultices, and tied them on my bones. "We need lamb skin or goat skin to wrap around your body, but I don't have any…"

I screamed all night from the pain. In the morning, she replaced the dressings. At noon, her husband, who had been away on business, returned. Seeing me in bed, he asked his wife:

"Who is this?"

Osgeg told him my story. I could see from the bed that the Kurd's expression changed. He seemed unhappy. He said nothing else and didn't even acknowledge me. He simply ate his meal and walked out.

This impressed me as a bad omen. A new pain was added to those I already felt. That Kurd, who had been raised eating at our family's table and enjoyed a thousand favors from my parents, was now giving me the cold shoulder when I had come to his home, half-dead, seeking help.

I threw off the blanket, I removed the poultices from my body, and said:

"Osgeg, I'll leave immediately. I don't care if I perish on the road."

She said nothing. She didn't try to hold me back or stop me. Clearly, she didn't want me to stay, either because she was scared of her husband, or because she, too, had become poisoned against Armenians after being away from them for so long.

I bade her farewell and set out. I took two steps forward, then looked back, and saw Osgeg weeping with her handkerchief held to her eyes. I stopped. She approached me, sobbing, grabbed my hand, looked into my eyes, and wept even more:

"I wished I'd gone blind before seeing you in this condition. I haven't seen an Armenian face for six years. I've gone mad with longing. And today, one of my own blood, of my own race, a man at death's door, falls into my lap, and I cannot talk to him, shelter him, and slacken my longing!

She wept so intensely that I couldn't stand it. I, too, began crying. We cried together.

"Bless me, Missak," she said, "this will be our last meeting. You will go and join Armenians again and forget me. But I won't forget you. This meeting has caused me grief. There is a new fire in my heart and it is burning me. Missak! Missak! Don't forget me when you leave these places and find yourself in distant lands! Remember that you have a wretched sister who is still suffering and burns in the flames of longing …"

This was the last time I saw Osgeg. I don't know if she has kept her vow to remember me…

After leaving Osgeg, I took the road to Kharpert and walked to Sarukhamish, three hours from Turkhe in the foothills of Mount Masdar.

I thought of going into Sarukhamish and of staying with Baghdoyents Margos for a few days, just to rest. Margos, like me, had fled the abuses of Hashim Beg and had settled down in Sarukhamish. He owned a tannery.

I stayed with Margos for a week. They took proper care of me and I recovered quickly. Then I proceeded to Kharpert. I visited my brother, who was in the orphanage of Hiuseynig. Then I visited the Prelacy and met with bishop Kiud [Mkhitarian] (no longer serving). I asked him to accept me into the Prelacy.

He had 400-500 orphans under his care, all of whom had escaped from the Kurds. The American orphanage, in order to avoid headaches, would not accept women and children who had escaped from the Kurds. This was because powerful Turkish begs and aghas would cause problems and threaten them for the return of orphans. But Bishop Kiud was well-respected in Kharpert and had influence on Turks. He was an old acquaintance and friend of the governor. He was an unparalleled prelate, a great patriot and diplomat. Many Armenian women and children owe him their lives.

One or two weeks later, after much wandering, Markar also made it to

Kharpert. I presented him to his holiness and he too was taken into the Armenian orphanage.

We stayed in the orphanage for another 10-11 months. In the autumn of 1922, we were forcefully deported by the Kemalists.

The American orphanages began evacuating in groups. My brother left Kharpert with the first caravan. The orphans in the Armenian orphanage, which included grown up boys of military conscription age, were the last to leave. I have no idea with what evil intent the government did not want these older boys to leave. But Bishop Kiud secured their free passage, too.

We left with the last caravan. It consisted of 800 people, including some Americans.

We traveled for 22 days. On the 23rd day, we reached Aleppo. It was the month of November. After two days in Aleppo, they separated us, and sent us to Beirut. Those who had relatives in America were kept in Aleppo so that they could write to them and ask for money. This way, they wouldn't be a burden on the orphanages.

In Beirut, on the shores of the Mediterranean, in the Lebanese mountains, in Jebel, Nahr Ibraham (Abraham's Bridge), Mamletein, Junieh, Antilias, Ghazir, all over the place… They rented buildings and built wooden sheds, where they placed the refugee orphans from Kharpert, Malatia, Gesaria, Cilicia, Konia, Marash, Urfa. I ended up in Nahr Ibrahim.

But soon, the orphans were left to their own devices. Some fell victim to an indolent Arab lifestyle; others fell from grace and lost their virtue. Those who were gifted with an iron will and a strong character returned to the lap of the Armenian nation and became part of the nascent Armenian community.

After the closure of the orphanages, and with supreme sacrifices, I was able to obtain enough money for ship fare. On May 15, 1925, I threw myself upon French shores and settled down in Marseille.

It was my father's will that I survive. He willed me to liberate myself, grow old, remember my family, and remember how they died.

Let this book be my modest contribution to my father's legacy, dedicated to the countless martyrs of the Armenian nation.

PALAHOVID

A Historical Overview

A Bit of History

Palahovid has a remarkable history. Due to their isolation for centuries, the people of Palou developed their own local character and temperament. As far as Armenian history has recorded the history of Palahovid, we can truly see that its traditions and customs differ greatly from other Armenian provinces and regions. It is not the entire region of Palou that was different, but each subdistrict and village, a short distance from each other, which spoke different dialects. This was because of the persecutions it suffered due to the region's political and geographical positioning. The region had fallen into the hands of a mob of different races and each Armenian village had to isolate itself.

Palou was not influenced much by Byzantine civilization. The Byzantine Empire reached Melidine (Malatia) and extended towards Kemakh (Ani). Palou was located on its north-eastern borders and always retained its independence. But the result of this independence was the *danouder* [patriarchal] system, which lasted to our days since time immemorial. Each *danouder* behaved as he wished and dispensed justice. Nobody could intervene.

The people of Palou, both Armenian and Kurdish, reverently and fearfully obeyed and served their masters. They treated their overlords as deities, as second gods. Nobody recognized the authority of the government. There was no proper administration, anyway. This explains why there were no reports written by any government department about Palou's past, nor any kind of serious historical studies. We only have some fragmentary information from the past, and even that information is difficult to access. The only vestiges of Palou's long history are the surviving traditions and mores of its people – their collective social, religious, political, and moral beliefs and customs.

Although the lords of Palou (i.e., the *amiras*) were Kurdish, they were of Armenian descent and fine models of ancient Armenian nobility. This is confirmed by historical facts, as well as the people themselves. Their customs and social mores were identical to those of Armenians. They had lost their Armenian identities for different reasons and had to become Muslims, a mixture of Kurds and Turks. Many of them did not even consider themselves Kurdish, and often denigrated Kurdish people. This class of amiras identified more closely with Turks because Kurds did not have a state, were not a nation, and had no government. They therefore considered it shameful to be called Kurdish. Most of them were begs and beys who lived in cities and denied their ethnicity. But if they ever became a little angry and excited, they would immediately cry out, "You know, I have Kurdish *damar* (vein)! Be careful! I have Kurdish blood, etc."

There were also different sects among Kurds. The two principal clans among these Kurds were the Hanefis and the Ghafayis. Although both groups were Muslim, they had both converted reluctantly to maintain their tribal (or racial) survival.

So, when we discuss the history and culture of Palou and its people, we must remember that the Kurds also had Armenian roots with the same traditions and culture. Perhaps they differed slightly when viewed from a religious perspective, but they were clearly the same people who had the same lifestyle. And although the Kurds committed the worst of atrocities during the massacres of Armenians, this was the result of their deep-seated ignorance. They reviled Turks and at the same time despised Armenians. Just as bats flee from light, Kurds fled from education. They were merely aware that they were Muslims by religion and Kurdish by ethnicity. They had no idea of their origins, or their destiny, or their purpose or end. They clung to the traditions that they had inherited from their ancestors, preserving their sacred rites and their ethnic character.

So much for Kurds. It was necessary to speak of them, as they lived side-by-side with Armenians of Palou and had a profound influence on their history.

Palou was divided into two sections – the upper villages and the lower villages. These villages faced each other across the Aradzani River. Arranged like beads, they seemed to be in conversations with each other. But the Aradzani had cut such a deep chasm between them that these people, who lived in the same province, had different traditions and peculiarities on either side. They related more closely and kindly with those on their side of the Aradzani river than the other.

The upper villages were in the area known as the Ashmoushad area.

The word Ashmoushad may have been a corruption of the word Ashdishad, although Ashdishad is in Daron. The Armenian and Kurdish villages of Ashmoushad also had their own unique characteristics. The Ashmoushad area was a large area and its northern belt stretched all the way to Moush, Sasoun, and further afield in terms of trade and architecture. At this end, that is, on these banks of the Aradzani, the villages can be divided into two. While Armenians occupied the flatlands and practiced agriculture, the Kurds, who held the mountainous regions, remote tracts, rocky crevasses, mountainsides and peaks, were sheep-herders. The mountain climate was very salubrious and people living there were energetic, healthy and hardy. Many of the Kurdish villages had Armenian names. Many had traces of temples and other pagan-era structures, such as Kharachor, Smsarkis (Sourp Sarkis), Miarvan, Oshin, Anato, Meghrapert, etc. Miarvan was in the direction of Hayni and Dikranagerd, while the aforementioned Oshin was only half an hour away from Baghin and Srin. One wonders how these two villages, Oshin and Baghin, remained surrounded by Kurds on all sides. Baghin was so mountainous and rocky that one could not plant the smallest amount of crops. However, Srin was a little more temperate and productive. Bagin was seemingly high in the skies with freezing winters. It was cold even in July and fruits did not ripen. The sun shone for two or three hours on Baghin. It was as if there were four pyramid-like mountains around it, with the village sunk between them. After Havav, Baghin was the only other sizeable and entirely Armenian village with its 120 households.

The Armenians of these two villages spoke a dialect that did not relate to any of the other Armenian dialects of the region. This was a dialect entirely of their own and deserves serious study.

Who has not come across that page of history which is called Baghin of Til, or Baghin's Til? Til has been the residence of Armenian princes. If we know this much, then we know that the inhabitants of that village were the descendants of exceptional people.

Among the lower villages of the plains were Til, Turkhe and Najaran with their mixed Armenian-Kurdish populations. These villages barely had a population of 35-40 households. This was the number of Armenians in Ashmoushad, but it is their quality that mattered more than their numbers. The people of the upper villages were more manly, proud and honest, civil and hospitable. Despite their deep Christian faith, they had a more noticeable pagan streak, which could be seen in so many Christian holidays. The traditions of pagan Armenians have left enduring traces among the people of Palou, especially around Ashmoushad. People in the villages continued to believe in *alk*s [daemons], *jin*s [genies], and *peri*s [fairies]. They would burn a candle and keep a watch over the bed of a new mother for forty days after childbirth so that the daemons would not be able to abduct their child and rip out the mother's liver with their copper fangs and iron claws. Their celebration of festivals was also more pagan than Christian. For example, during *Vartavar* [Feast of Transfiguration] and *Deyarentarach* (*melemed*) [Candlemas], they would light a huge bonfire on the roof of the *melik*'s house [local Armenian noble family] using evergreen *tsrti* wood, similar to the fir tree, and dance around it. Wasn't this part of pagan fire-worship traditions that survived the ravages of *Lousavorich* [i.e. Gregory the Illuminator]?

Palou's traditions were complex and difficult to explain. Many pagan customs were hidden behind a Christian veil. Any martyr who had been killed for the good of his people or Christendom was considered a miracle-working saint. Both Armenians and Kurds would appeal to the martyr's grave when sick, taking a bucket of water with them and washing themselves on the grave, believing that this would cure various ailments. There were trees and springs that were named after individual saints. Often, when people fell ill or were crippled, or even contracted venereal diseases, they blamed it on the vengeance of displeased saints. They thought that they were cursed because they didn't cross themselves when passing by a saints' grave or plucked a leaf from a saint's tree.

The Armenians of Palou attributed family successes and failures to a hidden creature that lived secretly among them in their house. When people grumbled because of misfortune or failure, they would claim that "Good-fortune has left our home." "We don't have a *deovlet* [hidden creature]." "Our *deovlet* has turned its back on us." Similarly, when they reprimanded a child, they would say, "Child of *bedeovlet* [no-*deovlet*], *kheyrsuz chojoukh* [no-good child], you drove our *deovlet* away. Our blessings abandoned us…"

Some people thought that their *deovlet* was an antlered snake. To others, it appeared as a human figure clad completely in green and wearing a green *kulah* on its head. Its eyes were supposedly green and it had a white beard that reached its waist. This imaginary *deovlet* was said to live in the storeroom and would hide behind wine containers or *tsavar* [grain] stores.

These legendary spirits or snake-*deovlets* even visited barns and pastures and followed homeowners and servants while they went about their work. They watched their masters' conduct and morals. If the latter did not take good care of the animals and cattle, or if they did not properly clean their manure, the *deovlets* would not allow the children to fulfill their dreams or marry the girls they loved. But woe to the man who was guilty of bestial behaviour. His home would burn to ashes and its *bereket* would disappear that very day. They would be cursed with misfortunes.

The Armenians of Palou attached great important to family traditions, just like Armenians in other Armenian inhabited provinces.

The people of Ashmoushad were particularly fanatical from this point of view. On the opposite side of the Aradzani, to its north-west, women were a little freer and bolder. Perhaps this was because many of their menfolk worked away from their province [*bantoukhd*] and the women were more empowered. The men often went to Constantinople, Cilicia and America and returned with more broadminded ideas. However, no men went away from the Ashmoushad area. They did not even go to work in Kharpert or Dikranagerd, let alone distant countries. The only exceptions were the villages of Baghin and Srin, which did not have land to cultivate and produced good craftsmen who had to make a living away from their villages. They were good *khizarjis* [woodturners] who made buckets and all sorts of wooden bowls. These were the men who first set off to the United States and returned with marvelous stories about the New World. But their family lives did not change in any way. They remained extremely conservative in their habits and customs.

As for the Kurds, the idea of migration was alien to them. They were indigent and had no marketable skills, so they simply kept sheep and goats and lived on their milk, cheese, and curds. They never ate wheat bread. They lived on *gulgul* and corn bread. They obtained these cereals from the

Armenian peasants. Some worked as servants, others made a living by theft or other means. They had no interest in wheat. Corn and *gulgul* were cheap and they would either buy or barter for it. In the winters, they would fry the cereals and survive on them until the mulberries and fruits ripened.

They would descend from the mountains, live on mulberries, and sleep in the open. They slept in gardens, under mulberry trees, and nobody would complain. There were many *kheyratluk* mulberry trees, which did not belong to anyone, but had grown wild or had been planted by kind hands on the side of roads.

The people of Palou had an anecdote as follows:

"One day, a Kurd comes to buy *gulgul* or corn from an Armenian peasant. He's shown a sample of each. The Kurd tries the samples and says, 'This corn looks good, but I can't buy it. I see a few grains of wheat mixed in it.'"

Despite living under such primitive and hardy conditions, Kurds never tried to seek work elsewhere. They clung to their homes and their families. Living alongside Armenians, they adopted Armenian customs. There were some Kurdish servants who not only knew Armenian, but had even learned Armenian prayers and church ceremonies.

Anyhow, the people of Ashmoushad never went away to work and lived well alongside each other.

The three Armenian lowland villages of Til, Turkhe and Najaran did not follow the example of others and preserved their own hallowed traditions.

The modesty and humility of the village women was such that no girl went away in marriage to another village. Fellow villagers had the right to stand up for any girl whose parents wanted their daughter to marry an outsider.

Only when a girl did not uphold traditional values and had various shortcomings would she be allowed to marry outside the village. And if she caused trouble in her in-law's house, they would remind her:

"If you'd been a good girl, they wouldn't have let you out of your village."

The people of Ashmoushad would never marry girls from the lower villages on the other banks of the Aradzani.

"They can't be our brides. The girls from the other side of the river are *chavoush*es [sergeants]."

There was one woman who had come to our village as a bride from the lower villages. My fellow-villagers would not utter her name, nor the names of her in-laws. They would refer to her as "the one from across the river."

***

Hundreds of thousands of people had crossed Palou bridge, whose magnificent structure had withstood the raging currents of the Aradzani for centuries. The colossal pillars of its seven-arched bridge rose high above the water. At that spot on the Aradzani, all the river's strength was channeled into a narrow gap, but elsewhere the river was broad and flowed peacefully. From a distance, you could see the waters seething with a hiss and coiling like a snake, then crashing against the bases of the seven columns. But the bridge always stood firm and victorious and never yielded.

Whose mind had devised it? Whose hands had built it?

The struggle between the bridge and the Aradzani was witnessed by the fortress of St. Mesrob, right next to the fortress, 10 or 20 meters away.

That fortress was as mysterious and miraculous as the bridge and the Aradzani.

Thousands of years earlier, when the brave army of Dikran the Great opposed the huge Roman army (of Lucullus), Dikran was betrayed by his own allies. The Armenians dispersed and Dikran retreated towards the Aradzani to the east. He then regrouped his men at Palou and routed the Romans. This was a battle to the death. The Romans were defeated and cut down by a handful of Armenian warriors. The Romans then sued for peace. One of the conditions for a peace treaty was the construction of Palou bridge. Dikran the Great forced the Romans to build it right where he had defeated them.

Next to the fortress of St. Mesrob was a cavern or bottomless pit called Kit (Kntig), which seemed like an abyss. It actually extended underneath the Vari Tagh [Lower Quarter] of Palou to the banks of the Aradzani. The opening was covered by a huge rock called Nounig.

This passage had been built for two reasons. First, if the city were surrounded, people could make their way to the river and fetch water from the Aradzani. Palou otherwise suffered from a lack of water. The second and more plausible purpose of the passage was to move military forces undetected to surround enemies by surprise and cut them down.

The city of Palou was attacked and sacked many times by barbarian tribes.

Palou's forts were held for many years by Arab *amiras* and princes.

Palou had huge forests that stretched towards Sasoun.

END

Melkon Gurjian

Melkon Gurjian, known by his pen name Hrant, was born in September 1859 in the village of Havav of Palou, where he received an incomplete primary education. Having a great thirst for learning, he traveled to Constantinople in 1870, where he attended the lyceum of Uskudar until 1875. He was a classmate of Mihran Tourian (the future Archbishop Yeghishe Tourian). After leaving the lyceum, he enrolled in the Sourp Khach [Holy Cross] School. He was a pupil of the well-known Armenologist Khachadour Misakian.

From 1878 to 1896, he worked as a teacher, teaching Armenian language (both classical and modern), literature, and history.

During the Hamidian massacres of 1896, he was in Constantinople. Hearing that he was being sought by the authorities, he was able to hide for several months thanks to his friends and acquaintances, eventually escaping to Varna [Bulgaria], where he founded the Ardzrounian School alongside Miss Armenouhi Minasian.

In 1898, believing that the situation in Turkey had stabilized and that the events of the past were forgotten, he returned to Constantinople. However, upon stepping foot in the city, he was arrested, and after a six-month prison sentence, exiled to Kastemouni [Kastamonu].

After the reinstatement of the Ottoman Constitution, in 1908, he returned to Constantinople, where he continued to work as a writer and teacher until the Armenian Genocide. In 1915, he was arrested alongside other Armenian intellectuals in the Ottoman capital. He was deported to Ayash and was martyred at the age of 56.

History and Traditions

Short Remarks on Palou

The name of Palou seems to be of ancient origins. According to historians, it probably originated with the name of Pahl, an ancient God, or the name of a prince. An alternative explanation is that the Palou area featured many forests of *palud* [cherry] trees, and over time, the *d* was dropped, and the area came to be known as Palou. This is the view held by many etymologists.

Palou has a long history that spans many centuries. But its past is shrouded in fog, and there are few reliable primary sources providing accurate information.

According to Pilador, "In the 19th year of the Hijaz (640 CE), local princes allied with the Romans included, other than the lords of Amida, the lord of Ariyavash (Kevork Gibratsi) and Sghert, as well as Sarvant of Arjish in Khlat, Khva and Salamas. Also from these lands, to the west, Prince Sanasar of Sasoun, whose son Daroun is called Moush in legend; Prince Pagour, also from the family of Prince Sarvant of Khlat, the lord of the forts of Patlis, Gafontor, Maden, Heyzan, Danza, Pedasa, and Arghn. Also the lord of Hiusn-Geyfey from the area of Hagaratsvots; and finally, Andiochos, who was the lord of Mavghe, except for the region between the city of Nprgerd to Heni, Jabaghchour, Dulgarne (near the wellspring of the main city on the Tigris), and Palou."

So, according to this source, Prince Sanasar of Sasoun and Prince Pagour from the dynasty of Prince Sarvant of Khlat ruled the fort of Palou.

Another historian, Parepreos, provides information that agrees with our theory that the name of Palou originated with its forested landscape. He writes:

"Under Arab rule, in 848, a Prince Pakarad, whose seat was in Moush, ruled the territory stretching all the way to the lands of Amit. When the cathedral of Amit burnt down, Pakarad donated 3,000 *chugha*s to the priests. In addition, he provided a huge amount of lumber for the reconstruction of the church…"

At the time, it was said that the highlands of Khouyt, Sasoun, Daron, and Jabaghchour were covered in huge forests. Such trees can still be found in the environs of Kinch, Jabaghchour and Palou, while the forests of Sasoun have disappeared.

After providing this information, we must emphasize that the history of Palou is still a great mystery and in need of much research and scholarship.

Islamized Begs

According to Islamic law, land belongs to God and his steward on Earth, the sultan. Islam's precept of "no princes, no beggars" also means that there is no nobility or class, and no ownership of private property, just an egalitarian society.

But the sultans of Turkey, who had concentrated all power in their hands and were viewed as the stewards of the prophet, bolstered the feudal system in the provinces by rewarding whomever they wished with land and titles, thus creating an aristocratic class. As a result, there were two sources of authority across the Ottoman Empire, one being the Sublime Porte, and the other being the feudal landowners, whose authority pre-dated that of the sultans. These begs, the descendants of Christian princes, had become apostates and had converted to Islam to retain their landed rights.

These hereditary chieftains constituted, one might say, a type of nobility of blood or sword, resembling that of ancient Armenian princely houses.

These were the feudal begs who ruled Lesser and Upper Hayk, the land of Dzop, Palou, Charsanjak, Kughi, Garin, Van, and Moush.

All the Armenian-populated provinces were ruled by these powerful despots who had the reins of government in their hands. Overlords, despots, bloodthirsty. They were the adjudicators in all regions. They ruled as they wished. They took over abandoned Armenian national properties *(vakf)*. If an Armenian died and left behind only a widow and daughters, they would step in and divide the deceased man's land and properties between themselves. The poor widows and orphans, deprived of their property, would have no choice but to emigrate or die in misery. Hashim and Teffiur Begs of Til were such despots.

Some Examples of Traditions

The Armenian people respect their traditions. They saw all of their highest national values in their religion. Armenians thought religion and nationality were the same thing. For ordinary Armenians, faith was a standard by which they measured everything.

The grave of a martyr was a holy site, the ruins of a church a pilgrimage site. A centuries-old tree, whose age was lost to the fogs of time, was no longer a mere tree, but a *srpadzar* [holy tree]. Every passer-by would tie a length of thread, a rope, or a kerchief to its branches, in hopes of being cured of various pains and ailments, or atone for their sins. There were also *srpaghpiur*s [holy springs]. People would bathe in them in hopes of being cured of fever, typhus, and various other diseases. After bathing in the waters, they would leave eggs, money, or wheat in the water-stream not to offend the holy spring.

O, Armenian nation, your faith is unshakable. You put your faith in the rocks, the trees, in miracles, and in the intervention of saints. You were happy because you had faith. Pity those who have no faith!

Despite Christian persecutions, the Armenian nation never abandoned its pagan traditions.

Navasart was the favorite of all holidays on the pagan Armenian calendar. It was held on August 15. To honor the God of harvest, Armenians would offer their first harvest of grapes to him, as a token of gratitude.

And now, the Christian Armenian church has replaced this ceremony with that of the blessing of the grapes on August 15, on the Feast of the Assumption of Mary, because Christianity was not able to erase that sacred celebration. It was this holiday that Ardashes the Conqueror referred to when he said, "*O dayr ints zdzukh dzkhani, yevCurdy zaravodn Navasarti, zvazeln yeghants yev zvakeln yeghcherouats, mek pogh haroudk yev tmpgi harganeak.*" [Who will give me the smoke of smoke, and the Navasartian morning, the running of the deer, and the whirling of the stags, while we blew trumpets, and beat drums.]

And what was February 14? In material terms, it was when they lit bonfires, around which new brides and grooms would hold hands, dance and rejoice. Up to the *Medz Yeghern*, Armenians in many villages, especially those of Palou, would hold these same celebration on the eve of *Dyarunharach* [Candlemas].

Starting from pagan times to the 5th century, the people of Armenia had no schooling or education. The only thing they could learn was catechism. Even after the invention of the Armenian alphabet, which led to the creation of institutions of learning across Armenia, most Armenians proved indifferent towards education and enlightenment. Learning remained the preserve of the clerical class and a small group of aristocrats.

As a result, Armenia did not produce true ethnographic historians who could separate history from tradition and legend so that the Armenian people could know their rights and culture without any doubts or misgivings. Without, that is, becoming skeptical or pessimistic about national values.

If Armenian children had been taught the history of their people properly, their teachers would have whispered to them that the story of Hayg Nahabed was legend, that the story of Ardashes the Conqueror was of doubtful accuracy, that Vahakn was none other than the Greeks' Ares, that Aramazt was none other than the Romans' Jupiter and the Greeks' Zeus, that Krikor Lousavorich (Gregory the Illuminator) was Parthian or Persian, etc.

Anyhow, who are the Armenian historians? Greeks, Romans, Assyrians, and Arabs, who wrote from their own whimsical and partisan position.

For example, Pavsdos Piuzantatsi praised foreigners but, when the turn came to Armenians, he cast suspicion on their victories and demeaned them for their false steps. He derided them in a really venomous manner. Read his works and you will understand what I mean.

Agathangelos and Pavsdos Piuzantatsi were Hellenes. They were better acquainted with Hellenic history than Armenian history.

As for Movses Khorenatsi, his source of information was Maribas Gadina [Mar Abbas Catina], who has been discredited by modern scholars. Regardless how unbiased foreign chroniclers may be, they can never truly capture the Armenian spirit and experiences.

Some Examples of Traditions

Pavsdos did not write an authentic history. He wrote on the basis of faith, about miracles, and the Holy Spirit, as in the revelations and visions of John the Baptist.

Revelations and visions are not history.

This is what historians say:

"The issues related to Pavstos Piuzantatsi are threefold: what was his nationality? What language did he use to write his history? Are the extant copies of his work complete or only partial?

"There are also other views on him.

"For at the end of the third book (Chapter III) he is called a Greek chronicler... And our Gahzar Parpetsi called him a Byzantine from the city of Byzantium.

"And there are other testimonies in our possession.

"For he himself was the chronicler of the Greeks at the time of the passing (Heading III)... And our Gahzar Parpetsi invited him from his native Byzantium.

"Other solid sources also establish that he also criticized the Armenian nation."

"As for Chamchian, he criticizes Pavsdos harshly:

"He may have been only of half-noble ancestry and not of great intelligence, for the language he uses is too vulgar even for common men, let alone the learned. Putting aside his terrible habit of repeating words and ideas, he distorts the timeline of history by stretching events that spanned only 20 years to over 50 years or more. His writing, his unsettled style, and his propensity for exaggerations lead readers to doubt his reliability."

And thus, the true history of Armenia has not been presented to us in its true richness. Every fact has been obfuscated to suit the temperament and whims of the chroniclers and historians. The events they recorded and the figures whose actions they chronicled depended on their own political and denominational interests. To this day, their histories are the subjects of lengthy debates among scholars.

Agathangelos was Roman by nationality but wrote his history in Armenian. Derendios Garketonatsi was absolutely proficient in Latin and had been educated in Rome, but preferred to write in Armenian. Pavsdos, meanwhile, still remains under critical debate.

The Monastery

The Apostle Thaddeus hatched many monasteries across the Armenian world. One of the monasteries he founded was located in our own village of Til and was named Sourp Khach (Holy Cross). The monastery's properties and estates were so extensive that pilgrims from a dozen different villages could stay there for weeks, eating, drinking, and enjoying themselves, without straining the resources of the monastery.

The monastery had fields, orchards, watermills, animals, every type of fruit tree imaginable in Armenia… It was like a Garden of Eden. Like a fearless and elegant queen, it sat on the summit of the mountain that faced the village. Through the trees, one could spot its millennial, dilapidated cupola, which looked like an ancient king's old crown robbed of its diamonds. Only the skeleton and supporting band remained. The monastery had a glorious history but was destroyed by the evil, destructive hand of the Turk in 1895. It had once had sixty different rooms, a library, museum, grape press and bake-house, all destroyed. However, they had not been able to destroy the cupola. I wonder what kinds of amazing architects had built it, and with what kinds of materials so many years ago, so that destructive hands had not been able to knock off even a picture-carving the size of a walnut. The barbarian race had failed in all its efforts to destroy the cupola.

This cupola had witnessed many crimes and massacres that had been committed over the years. Yet it stood strong and majestic into the 20th century, like the Armenian race, which had been persecuted and ripped apart, subjected to thousands of tortures, and attacked by armies of barbarians.

It matters not that the wealth of these monasteries and churches disappeared. But did the Turks ever realize that the power and creativity of the Armenian people was not restricted to the physical structures they had built? Its solid will and creativity was not limited to its deeds within four walls and miraculous creations. Its strength was in its spiritual substance that was of divine origin. It cannot be extinguished by neither sword, fire or the unimaginable and frightful exertions of barbarians. It will never be extinguished because its roots are lost in the mists of time. This is a nation that has produced great figures for the great ages and draped itself in great glories. From each drop of blood spilled, there will be a new Armenian who will raise a vengeful and glimmering sword and crush the skull of its inhuman enemy.

Sooner or later, the Armenian people will give birth to their God of Courage, their Vahakn, their "youth with the hair of fire," whose gaze will be the gaze of the sun, whose quiver will be filled with bolts of lighting, whose fire will come from the clouds, whose message will be from the stars, and whose weapons and finery will crush the chains of servitude and release Ardavazt from the depths of Mount Ararat.

MEMBERS OF PALOU COMPATRIOT

Standing, left to right: S. Chuchujian, M. Bzhian, B. Nersesian, H. Khojoian, M. Khralian, Kh. Chakoian, A. Manougian, H. Holopegian. *Seated, left to right:* H. Simonian, S. Simonian, B. Diradourian, M. Margosian, G. Diradourian, D. Vartian, H. Nigoghosian.

...NION IN MARSEILLE, 1938

Seated, left to right: S. Kghelian, M. Khralian, M. Kalousdian, S. Isrigian, H. Oulousian, Kh. Oulousian, M. Avoian. *Standing, left to right:* S. Khralian, K. Sarkisian, B. Koloian, G. Koloian, M. Baghdasarian, H. Markarian, D. Kalousdian.

To the New Generation

This little book of mine is a repository of memories, in which readers can find remembrances of my schooldays, an overview of my family's history, and a chronicle of the recent past. It is a record of the terrifying cataclysm of the obliteration of Armenians in 1915 (*1915i hayachinch sarsapnerou yeghererkoutiunu*), through which I lived under hellish conditions. It offers an overview of Palou's traditions, customs, mores and ways of a bygone era. It sheds some light on philology and studies, etc., which we have summarized as far as possible, to appraise the life of Armenians, especially in Palou, upon serious reflection.

In this book, tragedy and heroism walk side by side. In some cases I provided an overview of great events and figures in Armenian history because they created the greatness and glory of the Armenian nation. And since those times, the divine blood of Vahakn has been flowing through our veins.

We must look back at the mettle of our ancestors with pride and admiration. We must bow before their tombs with piety and reverence.

We need a new prophet to guide and lead the new generation to a new congregation.

Who will sound the clarion-call that will once again rally the Armenian people, scattered in all four corners of the world? Who will rekindle the flame in their hearts, the flame that has almost died out? Who will rekindle the fire of faith and hope of the embittered generation that survived in the burning sun of deserts?

Who will heal their wounds, and who will soothe their scars that are as deep as history?

The harp of the Yeghishes and Khorenatsis has fallen silent. New Yeghishes and Khorenatsis must pick up and sound the bugle that will revive the Armenian nation that has been dragged into a universal storm looming on the horizon. New Moseses must be born from the womb of this nation, capable of crossing red and stormy seas to a national Zion.

This generation is thirsty for the Armenian literary word and genius, but alas, our talented writers and thinkers have opted for adorning the bookshelves of their compatriots with translations and alien literature.

Where are the Raffis, the Kamar Katibas, the Nalbandians, the Beshigtashlians, and the Khrimian Hayrigs who can put the sparks of vengeance and patriotism in our souls and prepare this generation with an innate love of nation?

It is so terrible, after all these centuries of disappointments, to lose hope and surrender ourselves to powerful global currents … After such a valiant struggle, it is so hard to accept national expulsion, the tides of abandoned fate dragging us where they will.

Someone needs to witness my nation's terrible suffering and heroic struggle.

For this reason, such stories as my own must be written.

A single match is enough to start a wildfire. And such memoirs will serve as matches that start an inferno.

It is widely held that history is a golden thread that links the past to the future. It is history that teaches us of the former greatness and glory of the Armenian nation. It is history that teaches us our mistakes, that leads us to a more perfect path and a truer future.

We must also confess that history mercilessly exposes the truth and the enemies of justice. It separates light from darkness, good from evil.

Therefore, to write an objective account of the past is the duty of every person. Especially a past that has been condemned to be forgotten. A history full of bloodshed, carnage and the *yataghan*. A history in which even tombstones were not spared, so that in the future there could be no proof and liability that "Here rest the people of Hayg."

There are entire villages and regions reduced to ashes. Not even an insect was spared the sword, so that the world would not know that Armenians had once lived, prospered, and felt joy there.

Let people forgive us, if we cannot provide them with a profound analysis in such works. Let the reader be kind in his judgment and forgive us, bearing in mind that this is the diary and journal of someone who was 14 years old in the year 1915, who barely managed to escape the sea of blood and fire by a miracle. This is the story of a boy who came of age on the thorny and blood-stained paths of countless Armenians who were led to their deaths.

History teaches us what we have been and what has become of us.

For centuries, the entire Armenian nation has been suffering under the yoke of despots, plunderers, sardars, Seljuks, Tatars…

The journey of the Armenian nation into the 20th century has been a journey of loss of identity, of purification, of constant change, of evaporation, flight and of unsurmountable obstacles.

Alas! The 20th century! What a mockery!

The age of civilized humanity!

The century of new orders and new technologies!

The century of new gods and new idols!

The century of peace and justice!

The century of hope and faith, of renewal!

The year of the Lord 1915 – A historical watershed!

This is a chronicle of that year, written by a child of the times. It is a dirge and a requiem for a million unburied Armenians. It is a pantheon of the bones and relics of our elders.

Each Armenian has a duty to fulfill and a memorial to erect to keep the past eternally alive. Let this book be a modest shrine to those who gave their lives so that we may live.

GOMIDAS INSTITUTE ARMENIAN GENOCIDE DOCUMENTATION SERIES

Child Survivors

Missak Khralian, ***Palahovid: An Ancestral Memoir,*** translated from Armenian by Simon Beugekian; ed. and intro by Ara Sarafian, London: Gomidas Institute, 2021.

Hampartzoum Mardiros Chitjian, ***A Hair's Breadth from Death,*** London: Gomidas Institute, 2021 (2nd ed).

Vahram Dadrian, ***To the Desert: Pages from My Diary,*** transl. from Armenian by Agop Hacikyan; ed. and intro. by Ara Sarafian, London: Gomidas Institute, 2020 (3rd ed).

Souren H. Hanessian, ***Through The Depths: A True Life Story,*** London: Gomidas Institute, 2017.

Papken Injarabian, ***Azo the Slave Boy and his Road to Freedom,*** translated from French by Elisabeth Eaker, London: Gomidas Institute, 2015.

Jean V. Gureghian, ***My Father's Destiny: The Golgotha of Armenia Minor,*** translated from French by Diran Meghreblian with a preface by Yves Ternon, London: Gomidas Institute, 2015.

Avedis Albert Abrahamian, ***Avedis' Story: An Armenian Boy's Journey,*** edited with an introduction by Carolann Najarian, London: Gomidas Institute, 2014.

Levon Shahoian, ***On the Banks of the Tigris*** (Youth edition), transl. by Garabet K. Moumdjian, London: Gomidas Institute, 2014.

Euphornia Halebian Meymarian, ***Housher: My Life in the Aftermath of the Armenian Genocide,*** London: Taderon Press, 2005.

For more information on these and other titles
please visit *www.gomidas.org*
or contact *info@gomidas.org*

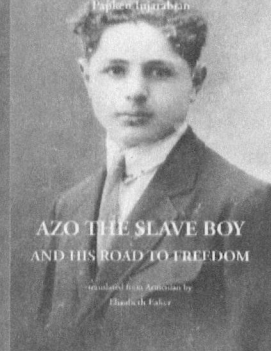

GOMIDAS INSTITUTE

www.ingramcontent.com/pod-product-compliance
Lightning Source LLC
Chambersburg PA
CBHW020052200426
43197CB00049B/373